Mostly
Mullet
Cookbook

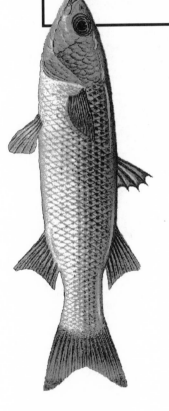

A Culinary Celebration of the South's Favorite Fish

The Mostly Mullet Cookbook

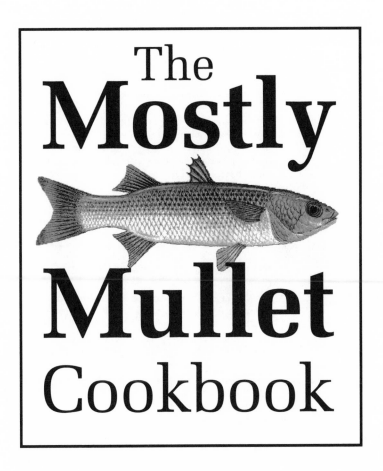

George "Grif" Griffin

Pineapple Press
🍍 Sarasota 🍍

Inquiries should be addressed to:
Pineapple Press, Inc.
P.O. Box 3899
Sarasota, Florida 34230

Library of Congress Cataloging in Publication Data

Griffin, George, 1932–
    The mostly mullet cookbook : a culinary celebration of the
    South's favorite fish / George "Grif" Griffin. — 1st ed.
       p.   cm.
    Includes bibliographical references and index.
    ISBN 1–56164–147–2 (alk. paper)
    1. Cookery (Mullet)   I. Title.
  TX748.M84G75 1997   97–45021
    641.6′92—dc21   CIP

First Edition
10 9 8 7 6 5 4 3 2 1

Picture Credits

Photos on pages 2, 3, 21—Florida State Archives
Photo on page 29—Florida Division of Tourism
Pen and ink drawing on page 5—Les Parbst, © George Griffin
Illustrations on page 8—courtesy of Old Salt Nets
Old engravings on pages 23, 31—Adgar Archives
Photos on pages 56, 57, 62, 64, 76, 81, 91 are by the author.
Other illustrations are from the author's private collection.

All logos and trademarks used are the property of their owners.

Sea dog illustration—FreeLantz Graphics

The mullet icon and related mullet designs used in this book
  were created by Octavo Design.

Design by Octavo Design
Printed and bound by Edwards Brothers, Inc.

Contents

Acknowledgments

First and foremost I must thank my spouse, Joanne, who has been both an inspiration (by her love of mullet) and a hawk-eyed proofreader on this project.

Other persons, groups, institutions and agencies who have helped with guidance, advice, recipes, and facts include: Hank Stoddard, D.V.M.; Leslie Sturmer, aquaculture specialist; John Falkenburry, mullet folklorist; Sue and Russ Colson, Florida seafood specialists; Gulf and South Atlantic Fisheries Development Foundation; Dot Williamson, Florida Bureau of Seafood; Marine Fisheries Commission; Bureau of Marine Research; Florida Department of Environmental Protection; and University of Florida, Sea Grant Program.

I have referred to literally hundreds of mullet references of which the following are among the more significant:

Atlas of North American Freshwater Fishes by Lee, Gilbert, Hocutt, Jenkins, McAllister and Stauffer, North Carolina State Museum of Natural History, 1981.

A Dictionary of Fishes by Rube Allyn, Great Outdoors Publishing, 1967.

The Ecology of Fishes by G.V. Nikolsky, translated from the Russian, published by T.F.H. Publications, Inc., 1978.

Atlantic and Gulf Coasts Field Guide by Amos and Amos, Audubon Society Nature Guide, Alfred A. Knopf, Inc., 1988.

The True South Mullet Cook Book by George "Grif" Griffin, Florida Mail Press, 1986.

"Fishing Lines, Anglers Guide to Florida Marine Resources," informational booklet by Florida Department of Environmental Protection, 1996.

Introduction: Why Mullet?

Why should a whole cookbook be largely devoted to the "lowly" mullet? Typically there are general cookbooks or even specialty books such as ones limited to fowl or seafood. But a book mostly on the thoroughly pedestrian striped mullet? Come on, now!

Well, the main reason for putting the mullet front and center is in recognition of the fish's unusual and delightfully nutty taste. No other fish tastes like a mullet. A commercial fisherman told me he compares the taste to a fresh pecan. "A pecan with fins," he said. Personally, I think mullet tastes something like sunflower seed. The taste is distinct yet subtle. But the fish must be prepared just right in order for this unique flavor to be appreciated. So, preparation is given much emphasis in this, our *Mostly Mullet Cookbook.*

There's more to the mullet than just its dandy taste, however. I get razzed all the time for my intense interest in, respect for, and preoccupation with *Mugil cephalus* (the striped or black mullet), a beautiful fish for which I have had genuine affection since my childhood. Growing up in Pinellas County, Florida, I enjoyed endless opportunities to see mullet in action and to eat them in any of several different forms, my favorite of which was smoked. In my childhood days, great schools of streamlined, silvery, torpedo-shaped mullet swarmed through the channels under the many bridges that linked greater St. Petersburg's numerous coastal communities. At those short bridges I often watched wide-eyed while sweating, long-sleeved fishermen "snatched" mullet, sometimes two at a time, on big, leaded "snatch hooks," rigged at the end of a long line of leader gut or wire attached to a hefty bamboo pole. The snatch hook, either treble or quad, would be allowed to rest innocently on the bottom of the channel or a few inches off the bottom. The great pole pointed downward off the bridge rail, ready to be forcefully yanked upward when mullet swam through. The fishermen could see them coming and would shout to each other, "Here they come! Here they come!"

The multiple-barbed, half-pound snatch would stab into the water again and again until one or more fish had been removed from the school moving through. The mullet schools were so large—hundreds of individuals in a single group—it was easy to spot them. I saw snatch fishermen leave the bridge, after a few hours, with 50 or more fish, in those days a commercial quantity. Their compatriots, giggers (who used gigs or harpoonlike spears), never caught as many.

Also, there were ardent mullet fishermen with cast nets. They threw those nets poetically. "It's not a sport, it's an art," I had it explained to me. The cast netters got more fish than the snatchers, but they usually had to get wet to do it. They had more success throwing their nets from the shallows of shorelines into pockets

and small channels than from the sometimes dizzying heights of bridges. The main fish species caught by the cast netters was mullet. Sometimes they were seeking mullet for bait. This practice still is common, especially in south Florida. Not only do humans love to eat mullet, many fish love to eat mullet. Among them are popular sport species such as marlin and swordfish. Indeed, the sport billfishing industry is so vast that mullet, the preferred bait, have frequently brought a higher price as prey than as human food.

As a kid, watching mullet being landed by the score by highly skilled netters and deft pole-wielders, I always was aware of how the school appeared still huge even after the catch. Tampa Bay area waters were very clear in those days. You could see a mullet school approach a bridge, many individuals jumping stupendously several feet into the air as they sped along, and you could watch the school swim through the pass and on into the bay or bayou or inlet where it was headed for the purpose of foraging. You could see the fish plainly as they swam under the bridge, and you could watch as the dark mass gracefully sped off into the mysterious distance.

When our family visited other coastal towns in Florida, the mullet were always there and I always eagerly looked for them, as

Jumping mullet, striped mullet, black mullet, gray mullet, the Spanish term, *lisa,* and the Latin *Mugil cephalus* all are names for the same delicious fish.

for old friends. Among our favorite spots were the Mud River and Weekiwachee, the first being tidal and salty and the second very fresh from a huge spring, now famous. Both were full of mullet, jumping mullet, day and night, rain or shine. At the Mud River, near Bayport, people sat on the decadent wooden dock and fished for mullet, using bits of algae or grubs or whole kernel corn for bait. Mullet would be jumping all around them. Some of the mullet anglers would chum them with laying mash (poultry food).

Meanwhile, a hundred miles north at the coastal community of Steinhatchee, mullet were taking their first look at a new kind of boat, the bird dog, invented in Taylor County, Florida, in the 1940s. This shallow draft design with an outboard motor situated fore, in a well, changed the future of mullet fishing. Bird dogs could go into much shallower water than normal craft and thus the fishermen could get on and around the schools more adeptly, allowing them to use long gill nets with extreme efficiency. For decades, this efficiency kept the price of mullet low and the quantity of the fish in the market high.

In the 1980s, demand from foreign markets drove prices of mullet up four to twenty times higher during the fall/winter roe season. In Japan and other Asian markets, mullet roe may sell for seventy dollars a pound and more. Unfortunately, the flesh of the mullet is wasted or used as crab bait when mullet are caught strictly for roe. Many Americans also enjoy the tasty, bright orange mullet roe, typically served "scrambled egg" style, but the home market never drove the industry the way the market in the Orient has.

Mullet were incredibly numerous in Florida and other Southern waters until recently. A decline was noticed both by scientists who are trained to watch for such changes and by others who watch mullet, as I do, as a fascinating pastime. In the early 1990s, Florida's Marine Fisheries Commission estimated that fewer than three out of ten adult mullet in southwest Florida's salt waters escaped fishermen each fall. Large Taiwanese business owners have been among major players in the mullet roe industry, which maintains an impressive fishing fleet and have been big financial contributors to the commercial fishing industry's resistance to regulation.

At the present writing the use of gill nets is highly regulated. As a result, the present price of mullet is more in line with comparable, high quality seafood. The fishing industry changes over the years, but thanks largely to restrictions born of research, mullet keep on jumping and jumping!

The fact that mullet jump often and for appreciable heights and distances is just one of the peculiarities of the species that endears it to us. Or, at least to me. I took early note of the mullet's jumping habit and also noted that most other species of fish do not jump unless hooked, racing forward on spawning missions, or otherwise disturbed. Exceptions include tarpon and sturgeon. I know of no other fish, however, that jumps nearly as much as mullet. And the mullet apparently jump for no better reason than the sheer delight of it.

When the species is healthy and abundant, mullet are jumping just about everywhere in the South's coastal or coastally linked waters. They also are jumping in the waters of Central and South America, off Africa and Australia, and just about any saltwater

environment where temperatures do not become too chilly. Generally, mullet favor a temperature range about the same as the author's preferences, from a low of about 50° F up into the 90s, the 70s being ideal. That's why we see so many mullet in Florida's cool, clear springs. Most of those springs flow at a temperature very close to 70. Manatees and mullet often are seen swimming together in spring runs. Both will tolerate swimmers, snorkelers, and scuba divers in very close encounters, almost with what could be called *friendliness*.

Mullet are identified as a marine species, but they can and do spend long periods of time in freshwater. It is common to see them well upstream in Florida rivers, the St. Johns system being one outstanding example. Most mullet gourmets agree, however, that mullet taken from salt water have a cleaner flavor than ones caught in freshwater. There is some debate on this point but not much. The final indicator of the mullet's true environmental orientation is where the species spawns. In the fall, thousands upon thousands of mullet take to the salty sea (as far as sixty miles offshore) where they create more mullet. One female generates a million or more eggs, most of which are eagerly consumed by other fish but not by the mullet herself. It is estimated that perhaps one in a thousand develops into a juvenile fish. These juveniles head for the coast, specifically for estuaries where they will feed and grow and feed and grow some more.

For many, many centuries, prolific mullet reliably reproduced in amazing numbers. And in the southern United States, especially the Gulf coasts of Florida and Georgia, mullet, abundant and cheap, became a staple on many a dinner table. Fried mullet or "salt mullet" and grits are credited with having got many a Southern family through the hard times as recent as the 1930s depression. Sometimes added to the mullet fare would be "swamp cabbage," the growth bud of a young sabal palm, a delicacy cooked or raw but not now such a good choice as palm forests are vanishing at an alarming pace. Hush puppies, ninety-percent cornmeal, were eminently affordable even for poor people, so they often accented the mullet meal as did the grits which even if buttered are just pleasantly bland enough to allow the fish's hallmark flavor to take the lead in the palatal event. This is why side dishes for mullet must be chosen with care and appreciation for the special taste which is peculiarly mullet.

It is, after all, the mullet's inimitable, eye-opening taste that causes anglers to go to great lengths to catch them, and chefs to endlessly toy with recipe possibilities to make them taste ever better, and some people to write books

about them. Millions of people eat them. Most will pay virtually any price. Yesterday, mullet was less than a dollar a pound dockside in the round. Today, the price is two to six times higher and demand remains strong. Commercial gill netting regulations (which could change before the ink is dry in this book) have made it tougher to take mullet in vast quantities, so the cast net is back in favor as is catching them on hook and line. Indeed, cast netting has become so popular both with commercial fishers and recreational anglers that an old and sinking industry has been reborn and revitalized. In Clearwater, Florida, Garth "Mutt" Gilliam and his family run a cottage industry called Cast Net King. Each year they supply tens of thousands of dollars worth of hand-tailored, monofilament cast nets to ready buyers throughout the mullet latitudes. Cast Net King offers nets as small as five feet in diameter and as large as twelve. There are many more net makers operating in the mullet latitudes, including Earc Hinz's Net Masters, just down the road from the author's hideaway in Old Town, Florida. Earc's specialty is heavy-duty nets in special colors. Some netters prefer certain colors, perhaps superstitiously, but with the claim that nets of some colors perform better than others. With mullet rebounding in population, the rising popularity of cast nets can be expected to continue.

Hook-and-line anglers' bait for mullet is usually plant life, such as small algae clumps, since mullet are basically vegetarian, but small pieces of fresh red worm work also. As mullet forage along the bottom and among aquatic plants, they unavoidably pick up some animal matter along with the green stuff. Which is to say, they don't reject a little pepperoni on their pizza.

It's important to know what mullet like to eat if you're going to try to propagate them. Seafood experts private and public agree that the demand for mullet is not going to subside. So, where there is a market there is an industry. Mullet can be raised in semi-captivity. Ancient Egyptians cultivated mullet in overflow deltas of the Nile. Texans have experimented. Some Floridians are looking seriously at aquaculture possibilities with mullet. This is good if you wish to eat mullet and are not able or inclined to catch your own. Commercial fishers using legal means will bring the fish to you.

And as you'll see later in this book, recent findings regarding the nutritional benefits of mullet make it even more important to make sure that a strong and vital mullet fishery remains and is cultivated in Florida's, the United States', and indeed all the world's temperate to tropical waters. Mullet is remarkably good food, quite easily obtainable.

OLD SALT

Mullet as Health Food

Of all the facts that have been discovered about mullet the best news is of the fish's amazing nutritional value. Not only does mullet taste good, it *is* good—good for you!

Mullet is a terrific source of protein—about thirty-two grams of the vital stuff to a single six-ounce serving of our favorite fish. Protein, bear in mind, is the number one essential item in a healthy diet. Protein is the backbone of cell structure. Humans do very poorly without it. We have to get it somewhere, and there are many potential sources, some better than others. Some proteins are incomplete and so are not efficiently utilized by the body unless combined with certain other foods. Fish supplies complete protein and, in the case of mullet, digestion and utilization of this protein is remarkably fast. Thus, a person who is low on protein nourishment could actually feel a protein "lift" after eating mullet. We dare to call it a "mullet high."

Consider: Even a modest four-ounce mullet fillet will supply nearly half the total protein required for an entire day by one adult human. The calorie count is only 170, and the fat may be about one gram per ounce of fish to more than double that in some specimens. Monounsaturated and polyunsaturated dominate the fat content, with saturated oil accounting for a third or less of the volume. That same fillet would be relatively low in sodium, averaging a mere 125 mg. What this data means is simple: Mullet is not only health food. It is healthy *heart* food.

An extremely important substance, Omega-3 oil, is present at a very healthy level in mullet, representing as much as twenty percent of the total fish oil present. One six-ounce mullet fillet could hold an entire gram or more of Omega-3, according to State of Florida documentation. Omega-3 oil has been proved to act as a protector against heart attacks and cardiovascular disease in general. Omega-3 is found only in a few sources, fish being the principal one. A survey conducted in the Netherlands showed a colossal reduction of fifty percent in fatal heart attacks among men who ate as little as one ounce of fish a day compared with those who ate no fish at all. A study from the Oregon Health Sciences University involved twenty men and women with dangerously high levels of cholesterol in their blood. Various health-oriented diets were used on these human guinea pigs, and it was happily found that all twenty enjoyed reduced cholesterol levels as a consequence. But the diet that reduced cholesterol the most (by almost half!) was the one with significant levels of Omega-3 fish oils. A small study at Harvard Medical School suggested that Omega-3 may actually prevent the build-up of fatty plaque in arterial walls. Many people take Omega-3 in capsule form and probably benefit from it. It takes about three 300 mg in capsule form to match the Omega-3 of one serving of fish. But no one doubts that if you live where fresh fish is readily available, well, the real thing beats capsules!

About five percent of a striped mullet's body weight is polyunsaturated oil.

Why does Omega-3 fish oil have such dramatic effects on human health? What does it really *do*? It helps to reduce the likelihood of clogs in the circulatory system. Science doesn't have all the answers about the precise mechanics of this effect, but study of the health histories of Eskimos have helped to establish it as fact. Despite the fact that they have high-fat diets, Eskimos practically never have heart attacks. Researchers have become convinced that the reason for this is all the Omega-3 Eskimos take in from the large amounts of fish they eat. The same has been found to be true in Japan and other parts of Asia where fish are prominent in the local diet. Where fish are eaten regularly, whether in Thailand or Hoboken, heart problems, especially heart attacks, are far less common. Apparently, Omega-3 tends to slow blood clotting. And clots, it is known, can be killers when they block flow to the cardiac pump. Pick up any health magazine on the newsstands today and you'll almost certainly find at least one story about the miracle of Omega-3.

Beyond healthy implications for the human cardiac system, Omega-3 apparently has several additional health benefits.

According to a twenty-four-week study at Albany Medical College in New York, rheumatoid arthritis sufferers who supplemented their diets with fish oil reported significantly reduced joint pain. And research at the University of Minnesota has shown that people who eat fish often are less apt to have bronchitis and emphysema. Some medical researchers have further observed that fish eaters are not as prone to depression as people who ingest little fish oil.

In the fish themselves, Omega-3 (derived from tiny plants they eat) seems to be one of the factors which allows aquatic creatures to remain supple, limber, and able to move and fan their fins even when water temperatures are so low that cold-blooded animals should be stiffly immobile. This same property may impart similar qualities when transferred to a person's vascular system, allowing the arteries to remain supple and clear of hardened obstructions. All of the answers are not clear yet, but there is no doubt about Omega-3's value in the human diet or about the mullet's role as a prime Omega-3 source.

In addition to mullet's richness in complete protein and Omega-3 oil, this deliciously wonderful fish supplies several additional substances and elements essential to human health. To name a few: vitamin A, vitamin D, calcium, magnesium, potassium, phosphorous, iron, iodine, fluoride, copper, zinc, manganese, cobalt, molybdenum, and selenium.

This last item, selenium, is present in significant amounts in most fish, including mullet, and in combination with Omega-3, may be responsible for fish's long reputation as "brain food." Selenium is believed to be necessary to the proper mix of human brain chemistry. Selenium also is winning a reputation with nutrition researchers for its

Mullet is so easy to digest that some doctors prescribe the fish for ulcer patients.

possible roles in strengthening the cardiovascular system and fighting cancer.

An apple a day may be classic health advice but an apple *and* a mullet a day would be even better. Among the many fantastic mullet recipes ahead you'll find one that does put the two together. Look for Mullet Apple Turbans on page 36. This might be the healthiest recipe in the book!

All of the recipes in *The Mostly Mullet Cookbook* are an adventure in good taste and have been made as healthy as we know how. Some of the more traditional recipes have been allowed to keep old-fashioned ingredients such as butter, but in reduced quantities; other recipes which once called for fat in the frying pan now ask for restraint even with unsaturated vegetable oils.

The idea is to supply recipes that turn out delicious mullet and are genuinely healthy at the same time. Good food, we think, can be *good tasting* food. So, each recipe for any of the several cooking methods stands on its own as a celebration of the South's wonder fish. Every recipe must be simple, health-savvy, and bring outstanding results for either practiced or novice cooks. That is this book's standard. The mullet is a champion fish of extraordinary quality, deserving nothing less then the best attention in preparation and cooking. So, let us now bring it that sincere attention.

Get ready for great eatin'.

 Of the marketed mullet, about 25% is sold fresh, 63% frozen in the round, 6% smoked and 6% as roe.

Preparing Mullet

We'll assume that you "caught" your mullet at the local fish market, supermarket or food store. As a general rule, the closer you are to the original source, the better.

If you're buying your mullet at the Winn-Dixie on the avenue and there's an operational, saltwater fishing village less than fifty miles from the store, you can take the "Fresh Mullet" sign seriously. But if you're shopping at Uncle Ferdie's Food-O-Rama and it's two hundred miles from the sea and the fish look tired from the trip, hold up.

The reason I say stop is because the way you acquire mullet is as important as the way you prepare and cook it. Indeed, acquisition is the most important step toward having a quality finished product you'll enjoy eating. This is generally true with fish, but more so with mullet in particular, since it is an established scientific fact that mullet remain in a fresh state for a significantly shorter time than most fish. We mentioned earlier about the limits for keeping iced or frozen mullet. But the rule is this:

Buy your mullet fresh.

Prepare and cook the fish as soon as possible.

SAME DAY preferred!

If you know you're going to cook and eat the fish within a few hours you may choose to have them cleaned and readied at the market. If you plan to freeze the fish almost immediately and save it for a few days, again, you may have the fish prepared where you buy it. Remember that you will always get the best cleaning and cutting job done at a true fish market rather than a general food market. If you intend to keep the fish around for more than a few hours but not more than eight, buy your mullet iced "in the round," i.e., whole mullet.

Mullet can be prepared in any of a variety of ways. How the fish is "carved" depends on the planned manner of cooking. A mullet

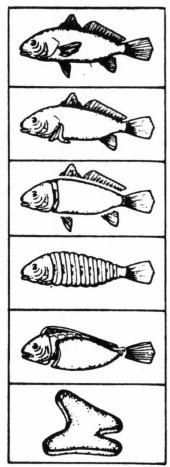

WHOLE OR ROUND Mullet are marketed just as they come from the water. They must be scaled and eviscerated before they are cooked. Usually, the head, tail and fins are then removed.

DRAWN Mullet has the entrails removed. They must also be scaled, and the head, tail and fins may be removed.

DRESSED OR PAN-DRESSED Mullet are both scaled and eviscerated. Usually, the head, tail and fins are also removed, and they are ready to cook when purchased.

STEAKS are cross-section slices of the larger, dressed fish. Most mullet are too small to make attractive steaks, but when they weigh 5 lbs. or more, they may be steaked.

FILLETS are the sides of dressed mullet cut lengthwise away from the backbone, and require no preparation before cooking. A really economical buy, they are almost 100% edible.

BUTTERFLY FILLETS are two sides or fillets of dressed mullet, held together by the uncut belly skin of the mullet. This form is popular for outdoor cooking.

to be smoked will be cleaned and prepared entirely differently from a mullet whose destiny lies in a frying pan.

Frying is the most popular method of cooking mullet and we start our recipe section with this traditional mode. So, most mullet is cleaned and prepared for frying. And this generally means filleting the fish with rib cage left in. The dark patch of belly lining is removed. For people who love mullet and prefer bone-free fish, mullet can be filleted with the rib cage removed.

For broiling and grilling, the fish should not be too small. Two- and three-pounders are perfect. Smaller fish can be merely beheaded and gutted, then cooked fins and tail on.

In this state, the mullet are called "drawn." But for all cooking methods, the starting point is the same: *There is a fish that needs to be converted into a product.* This may mean the use of a scaler or skinner and one or more knives, perhaps also a sharp tablespoon for working with that belly lining. Have plenty of cold water available and running.

As a general rule mullet are *not* skinned because their tender meat tends to fall apart easily when the skin is not in place. This is a point to remember when preparing and handling the fish. Some recipes call for skinned, and when that's the case, your best bet is to have the fish skinned at the market.

The mullet should be iced when they're being cleaned. Never should they be lying around un-iced, nor should they be allowed to thaw at room temperature. (A microwave may be used for a quick and safe thawing of frozen mullet.) The cleaning work should be bathed with fresh, cool water as necessary. Only very sharp, sterile knives should be used. The cleaned fish or fillets should go to a cold environment immediately afterwards.

One of the most popular ways of preparing mullet is the butterfly cut. Butterflied mullet is the two sides of dressed mullet held together by the uncut belly skin. This is a popular style for broiling mullet and is also popular for outdoor grilling.

An even more popular cut for smoking is the traditional split in which the fish is essentially cut from the dorsal down the middle, following the backbone, and laid open so the backbone is on one side. Sometimes this cut is done head-on, and in other parts of the South it's head-off. Usually, the tail and some fins are left on. For smoking, the mullet need not be scaled. For other types of cooking, it should be.

 When buying whole mullet, remember that one of the best indicators of freshness is bright eyes.

Large mullet can be steaked. We're talking about four- and five-pounders. The steaks are created by doing cross-section slices of the scaled, drawn, and dressed whole mullet. These steaks are ideal for grilling, broiling, or microcooking.

A mullet can be cooked by any method once it has been scaled and eviscerated. Any "whole" mullet being kept on ice longer than an hour should be gutted. Occasionally, it is desirable to cook a virtually whole fish, i.e., fish in the round. Such a mullet can be cooked on a spit over an open fire.

 The six best ways to cook mullet are smoked, broiled, grilled, fried, microwaved, and baked.

Mullet Insiders' Cooking Tips

Whatever method of cooking you may be using, the number one caution is *don't overdo it*. Overdone fish loses its flavor and natural texture. Since the taste of mullet is so distinct, yet subtle, it suffers greatly from overcooking.

Except for smoking, it is best to get the fish cooked as quickly as possible. This is especially true of frying since the longer the fish is in the oil the more oil will be absorbed, and a greasy mullet is a bad mullet. Microcooking is another process where a minute too long can be ruination since an overnuked fish is a rubber fish.

How to check: Lightly stab the fish with a fork; twist slightly. If the meat is opaque and it flakes readily, it's either done or mighty close to being ready. You do not want the meat to dry out or get tough.

As a general rule, mullet is cooked with skin on. Most mullet gourmets contend that the skin imparts essential flavors. More practical mullet maniacs admit that the skin's primary purpose is to help hold the piece of fish together. Mullet is very tender.

What's a portion? How much mullet is enough? I usually buy too many. A one-pound mullet will offer between eight and twelve ounces of meat, depending on the method of preparation and whether the backbone and ribcage are left in. For many people, three and a half or four ounces of fish is plenty. For others, it takes more, perhaps a lot more, to satisfy. You have to gauge the number of fish by the prospective appetites of your diners. For just a couple, let's say Joanne and me, two small mullet is the perfect buy.

A typical annual commercial catch of fifty million pounds of mullet could be produced by twenty-five mother fish if all their eggs developed into marketable adults.

Let's Cook a Mullet

Let's cook a mullet or ten or more.
Fat in the skillet's what a mullet's for.
It's the best eatin' fish from shore to shore.
Eat a piece, come back for more.

Fried

We start with fried because probably four out of five mullet consumed in the Western world *are* fried, either pan or deep, and almost everyone agrees that it's the epitome of mullet preparation. A delicately fried mullet fillet can be compared to the finest gourmet seafood items. Traditionally, fried mullet is served with steaming grits.

Among the fried mullet recipes which follow are several that come to us from an earlier day when we knew not the risks of lard and saturated and hydrogenated oils. In many cases we have modified the original recipes so they better reflect today's understanding of healthy nutrition. Modified does not mean compromised, however, and we believe that in most cases the lower fat recipes truly produce a better end product, i.e., the mullet itself looks better and tastes better. At the end of this section we supply additional hints for lowering the fat content of most seafood recipes still more.

Dixie Fried Mullet

This is a traditional fish fry recipe for which the quantities of ingredients will vary with the size of the group or family. Allow one to three fish per person depending on size of mullet.

Mullet fillets

Peanut oil

Salt and pepper

Cornmeal

Prepare mullet fillets into convenient, frying-sized pieces. Keep the fillets cold until ready to fry. Salt and pepper both sides of each fillet, roll in stone-ground yellow or white cornmeal. Fry the fillets *fast* at 375° F in peanut oil. Drain well on paper towels.

Serve with hush puppies and Dixie Red Sauce and/or tartar sauce. Also may be served with malt vinegar.

A variation of the above recipe uses an "egg wash" in addition to the cornmeal. The fish goes into the meal, then into the wash and back to the meal for a final roll before arriving in the frying pan. Fry the fish until pleasantly golden brown. It will flake easily with a fork when ready. Mullet fries fast.

Dixie Red Sauce

1 cup ketchup
4 tablespoons fresh ground horseradish
1 teaspoon Louisiana hot sauce

Mix ingredients thoroughly. Chill and serve with fried mullet or shrimp.

Simplicity Tartar Sauce

Same as served at many of the South's finest seafood restaurants

¼ cup mayonnaise or salad dressing (low-fat OK)
2 tablespoons sweet pickle relish

Combine ingredients, mixing well. Makes about ¼ cup of delicious, uncomplicated sauce that won't compete with the flavor of the fish.

Old South Hush Puppies

The traditional accompaniment for fried mullet

½ cup flour

1 cup yellow cornmeal

½ cup minced onion

1-½ teaspoons baking powder

1 egg

1 teaspoon salt

2 teaspoons sugar

½ cup milk

Oil such as canola, safflower, or peanut

Blend all ingredients except milk and oil. Stir in just enough milk to moisten dough. It's "right" when it's both stiff and heavy. Drop from tablespoon into hot (350° F) oil and fry until pleasantly brown, about 3-½ minutes. Traditionally, certain down-home, seaside eateries deep in mullet country such as Florida's Big Bend (try Roy's at Steinhatchee) serve their hush puppies with guava jelly. But most of the more commercial and franchised seafood spots don't even know how to make puppies the right shape! (They *should* be longer than high by a factor of at least two to one.) Makes about two dozen downright delicious hush puppies.

Cracker Mullet

1-½ pounds of mullet fillets

3-½ ounces of cracker meal

1 egg

2 tablespoons water

Crush from your own crackers or use a specially-prepared product such as Nabisco cracker meal, which has the advantage of no added shortening, making it stay fresher and fry smoother.

Pour cracker meal onto waxed paper. Roll the mullet fillets in the meal until they pick up a fine, even coat. Put egg and water into a shallow bowl and beat until blended. Dip crumbed fish into egg mixture; then roll again in the meal. Fry in deep fat or sauté in canola or safflower oil. Drain on paper towels. Serve piping hot. Enough fish for four.

Palatka-style Spudz Mullet

This recipe has become slightly famous.

1-½ pounds mullet fillets, fresh or frozen
1 teaspoon salt
¼ teaspoon pepper
1 egg, beaten
1 tablespoon water
1 cup instant mashed potato flakes
⅛ cup canola oil
1 ⁷⁄₁₀-ounce envelope dry Italian salad dressing mix

Thaw mullet if frozen. Sprinkle fillets with salt and pepper. Combine egg and water. Combine potato flakes and dressing mix. Dip fish into egg mixture, then roll in potato mixture. Place fish in a heavy frying pan which contains about ⅛ inch of oil, hot but not smoking. Fry at moderate heat. When fish is brown on one side, turn carefully (mullet is fragile) and brown on the second side. Total cooking time: 9 to 10 minutes, depending on thickness of fish. Drain on paper towels. Makes four servings.

 Several bird species, including pelicans, successfully catch mullet from surf and sea. One of the best mullet fishers is the osprey, a high-diving sea hawk which seems to prefer mullet over all other types of fish.

TAKING THE FAT OUT OF FRYING

While many of *Mostly Mullet*'s frying recipes have been adapted to lower fat standards, several appear essentially in their traditional versions which were authored before most people had heard the word *cholesterol.*

The trouble is, many fatty and cholesterol-rich foods happen to have full, pleasant tastes which human palates appreciate. Take butter, for example. Tasty. Even popcorn seems empty without it. Eggs, too. Eggs have a unique taste that many people can hardly live without. But for those who have become health-conscious, whether out of informed concern or doctors' orders, there are ways to have eggs and be healthy, too. This is especially true when either or both are serving basically functional rather than flavoring roles. Anything you can fry or sauté in butter would be as good or better in peanut, cold-pressed safflower, or olive oil—as long as you're careful not to smoke the oil. And in recipes where an egg is used to hold something together, like a breading or a hush puppy, two fat-free whites can be substituted for one whole egg with yolk. Give the yolk to your Australian shepherd; it will make the dog's coat shiny and help save your heart.

No recipes in this book call for palm or coconut oil since (although veggie) they're practically as artery-jamming as lard. If you find recipes calling for these products anywhere (and cottonseed is suspect as well) substitute olive, safflower, canola, soy or corn. Do not overfry. Get those fish out of the deep fry cage or frying pan *within 10 seconds of "done."* Every extra second is extra grease. The best way to learn how to get fried fish perfect is to practice a lot.

To make recipes that call for buttermilk more health-smart, simply choose the lowest fat variety. Buttermilks vary from 3.5% fat to virtually fat-free. Mayonnaise also now comes in both low- and no-fat versions. We have found *Smart Beat Non-Fat* to be a tasty, healthy choice

that can be used in tartar sauce and many other recipes calling for mayo. The same goes for sour cream and cream cheese; even the no-fat versions are surprisingly good. However, in our experience it pays to go with the more expensive brands.

When it comes to frying, here is a more complete list of the preferred oils, roughly rated in the order of preference: extra virgin olive, Smart Balance (a heart-wise oil blend by GFA Brand, cold-pressed safflower, peanut, sunflower, canola, corn, and soy. These oils, especially the first, also are excellent for use in salads. Speaking of salads. Here is the salad we rate as number one for serving with fresh fried mullet.

The 1906 Salad

Perfect with mullet (or any fried fish)

½ head iceberg lettuce

2 tomatoes, diced

1 celery stalk, diced

3 ounces low-fat Swiss cheese

¼ cup pitted Spanish olives

2 tablespoons low-fat Romano cheese

Arrange salad ingredients on four individual salad plates and dress with the following dressing.

Dressing for The 1906 Salad

Inspired by the famous Columbia Restaurant, where with great showmanship they dress your salad at your table.

4 garlic cloves, minced

1 teaspoon oregano

1 teaspoon Worcestershire Sauce

Juice of ½ a lemon

½ cup olive oil

⅛ cup white vinegar

Salt and pepper

Mince garlic and put in a bowl; add oregano, Worcestershire sauce and lemon juice. Beat with a wire whisk until smooth. Add the oil gradually and finally the vinegar, beating continuously. Add salt and pepper to taste. When well mixed, pour dressing over each salad and toss.

Beer-Battered Mullet

This recipe was developed for use with an outdoor, LP gas fryer. These frying machines have the advantage of putting the heat, fumes and mess outdoors. Also, they deep fry with great efficiency and speed so that not too much oil is absorbed. Gas fryers are sold by home improvement and department stores as well as by LP gas distributors.

2 pounds of fresh mullet fillets, skin on
½ cup flour
½ cup yellow cornmeal
1 cup flour
12 ounces premium beer such as Michelob or Old Milwaukee
1 tablespoon salt
1 tablespoon paprika
Peanut oil for frying
Malt vinegar (optional)
Important: Use two bowls.

In first bowl, mix ½ cup flour and yellow cornmeal. In second bowl, add 1 cup flour, beer, salt, and paprika. Blend well and let sit at room temperature for one hour.

Make sure mullet is dry. First dip fillet into dry mixture and then into batter. Shake off excess and fry in hot peanut oil in small batches until golden brown. Serve with malt vinegar. (You can buy excellent, by-the-bottle malt vinegars at most fast food fish chains or at the supermarket. A good brand is House of Herbs.) Serves six.

Rube Allyn's Spicy Apalachicola Mullet

Credited to the late, legendary Florida outdoor writer, Rube Allyn

2 pounds of mullet fillets
All-purpose flour
1 egg
2 tablespoons of yellow salad mustard
Table salt
Peanut or canola oil

Beat the egg thoroughly and add the mustard. Add a little salt to the mixture and stir together. Dip each fillet into the egg coating first and then roll quickly in flour. Fry at 375° F until the fish flakes easily with a fork. Drain on paper towels. Serve with tartar sauce to as many as six happy diners.

Tartar Sauce No. 711

Great with fried, baked, broiled or grilled mullet

1 cup mayonnaise

¼ cup reduced- or low-fat sour cream

2 tablespoons chopped dill pickle

2 tablespoons finely chopped onion

2 tablespoons chopped Spanish olives

1 teaspoon lemon juice

⅛ teaspoon black pepper

Combine all ingredients, mix thoroughly, and chill. Makes two cups of sauce that will get raves.

Deep-Fried Wine-Battered Mullet

This recipe was specifically developed for use with an outdoor LP gas fryer but works fine with any deep-fry rig.

2 pounds mullet fillets with or without skin

1-½ cup flour

1 teaspoon baking

Salt and pepper

White wine

Peanut oil

Mix flour, baking powder, and salt. Add enough wine to make a pancakelike batter. Cut mullet into individual-sized pieces and blot dry with paper towels. Salt and pepper the fillets and dip into the batter. Slip battered fish into hot oil in deep fryer and cook until golden brown, turning only once. Drain thoroughly. Serve with Dixie Red Sauce, tartar sauce, or vinegar. Serves six.

Deep-Fried Buttermilked Mullet with Lemon Relish

This recipe developed by state of Florida kitchens (devoted to healthy promotion of Florida seafood) is well worth the effort.

2 pounds skinless mullet fillets

1 cup low-fat buttermilk

1 cup biscuit mix

2 teaspoons salt

Peanut, canola, or safflower oil

Lemon Relish (recipe follows)

Thaw fish if frozen. Cut into serving-sized portions. Place fillets in a single layer in a shallow dish. Pour buttermilk over fish and let stand 30 minutes, turning once. Combine biscuit mix and salt. Remove fish from buttermilk and coat with biscuit mix. Place fish in a single layer in a fryer basket. Deep-fry in hot (350° F) oil 3 to 5 minutes or until fish is brown and flakes easily when tested with a fork. Drain on absorbent paper. Serve with Lemon Relish (next recipe). Makes six servings.

Lemon Relish

½ cup low-fat sour cream

¼ cup crushed pineapple, drained

2 tablespoons diced, peeled lemon

2 tablespoons finely chopped green pepper

1 tablespoon finely chopped onion

1 tablespoon light brown sugar

1-½ teaspoons grated lemon peel

¼ teaspoon dry mustard

¼ teaspoon celery salt

⅛ teaspoon ground cloves

Combine all ingredients. Mix well. Chill. Makes approximately one cup of awesome relish.

Lighthouse Hush Puppies

This recipe is from a famous seafood restaurant. To attempt to duplicate their tasty puppies, you'll need a mystical dash of Dixie flair.

2 cups self-rising cornmeal

1 cup self-rising flour

1 medium onion, finely chopped

1 teaspoon garlic powder (or to taste)

½ cup mayonnaise

½ cup buttermilk

½ cup sweet milk

Mix dry ingredients. Add onion, mayo, and buttermilk. Gradually add milk until batter is of medium stiffness. Let rest 30 minutes before cooking. Stir again. Using a teaspoon dipped in grease, spoon batter into hot deep fat (360° F) and fry until golden brown. Drain well on paper towels. The recipe supplied to us claims it will make exactly one batch but exact size of a batch is not given.

In Southern cooking, the hush puppy is an art form—like throwing a cast net.

Panafried Mullet from Panacea

This traditional recipe from Florida's Big Bend is not a simple one, but it is a good and old one that promises outstanding results if the ingredient list and procedures are followed precisely.

2 tablespoons regular white flour

¼ cup toasted bread crumbs

1 teaspoon dried tarragon

2 tablespoons grated Parmesan cheese

¼ teaspoon onion powder

¼ teaspoon salt

1-½ pounds mullet fillets cut to easy-fry size

2 egg whites beaten with 2 tablespoons low-fat milk

1-½ tablespoons butter or olive oil

2 tablespoons lemon juice

2 tablespoons chopped fresh parsley

Spread the flour on a shallow plate; a paper plate is fine. In a sizable shallow bowl combine the bread crumbs, tarragon, cheese, onion powder and salt. Roll each fish piece in the flour, then in the egg and milk, and quickly in the dry bread crumbs. Put aside. In a large nonstick skillet, heat the oil and lemon juice until it sizzles. Add parsley. Tilt the pan around to coat the frying surface evenly with the mixture. Reduce heat to medium, introduce the fillets, and cook each side for 3-½ to 5 minutes or until the fish is golden and done, but not dark brown. Makes four servings.

 There are several different species of mullet, including redeye, white and fantail, all of which are known as silver mullet. Red mullet of the Mediterranean is a species not related to our mullet.

Piney Woods Fried Mullet

Squirrels aren't the only ones who can enjoy the spicy little nuts that are inside pine cones. You can buy these nuts at larger vegetable markets and health food stores. To prepare the pine nuts, simply stir-toast them on medium high heat in a nonstick frying pan for perhaps two minutes. Set aside.

2 tablespoons pine nuts

1 pound mullet fillets

2 tablespoons yellow cornmeal

2 teaspoons butter

1 small onion minced

1 sweet red pepper cut in strips

1 teaspoon malt vinegar

¼ cup chicken broth

Sprinkle the mullet fillets with cornmeal. In a large frying pan, melt butter at medium fire; add fish and sauté until done, about 2 to 3 minutes per side. Remove fish and arrange on a serving dish. Add minced onions and peppers to the hot frying pan and sauté for up to two minutes before adding vinegar and broth. Gradually bring to a boil and simmer until liquid is reduced to half volume. Pour the broth over the fillets and top with pine nuts. Serve, and once again be prepared for spirited compliments. Serves two to four.

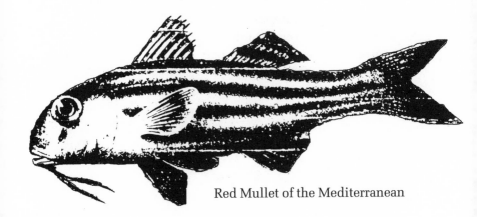

Red Mullet of the Mediterranean

Mullet Almandine

The state of Florida has developed many fine mullet recipes, and this is one of the very best among them. To bring a gourmet touch of elegance to what was until quite recently the "poor man's fish," you will need:

2 pounds mullet fillets

2 tablespoons lemon juice

2 teaspoons salt

⅛ teaspoon black pepper

½ cup all-purpose flour

⅓ cup butter, melted

½ cup blanched, slivered almonds

2 tablespoons chopped parsley

Sprinkle mullet fillets with lemon juice, salt, and pepper. Coat fish with flour. In a large fry pan, arrange fish in a single layer in melted butter; cook over medium heat for 4 to 5 minutes or until brown; turn and cook 4 to 5 minutes more or until fish is brown and flakes easily when tested with a fork. Drain on absorbent paper; remove to a warm serving platter. Sauté almonds in remaining butter or oil until lightly browned; add parsley. Serve over the mullet fillets. Makes six servings.

 In Mississippi, mullet has been nicknamed "Biloxi Bacon," and the fish sometimes is served crisply pan-fried for breakfast—with grits.

Baked

Because mullet has a good oil content and is naturally tender, it is an ideal fish for baking. Any conventional oven will do.

Many people, when they are offered "baked fish" instinctively shy away from it. Restaurant chains have not done well with the concept, although several have featured it. That's a shame because folks are missing out on a creative and healthy way to prepare fish. Baked mullet is deliciously different.

Here are some baked mullet recipes we think will surprise and delight you.

Brunswick-style Baked Mullet with Cape Cod Sauce

We have been told that each serving delivers less than 8 grams of fat and only a dab of cholesterol despite the butter, so we have left the ingredients intact.

Nonstick low-fat cooking oil spray

1 tablespoon butter and 1 tablespoon olive oil, mixed

2 tablespoons fresh parsley, minced

2 tablespoons shallots, minced

½ teaspoon salt

Black pepper

2 tablespoons lemon juice, fresh if possible

1-½ pounds mullet fillets from larger mullet

Preheat the oven to 450° F. Spray a baking dish with the nonstick coating. The dish should be large enough for the fillets to fit in a single layer.

To make the Cape Cod Sauce: Combine the butter mixture, parsley, shallots, dill, salt and pepper in a small saucepan. Heat over low heat, stirring occasionally until the butter is liquefied. Remove from the heat and stir in the lemon juice.

Position the fillets in the casserole and cover with the sauce. Bake for 9 minutes covered then 5 to 10 minutes uncovered or until done; test if necessary. Upon serving, spoon some sauce over each portion. Enough here for five or six persons.

Shrimp-Stuffed Mullet

A real production number. Don't attempt this recipe unless you really are ready for an hour or so of preparing a truly sensational meal.

6 bone-free fillets from larger mullet

½ cup lime juice, halved

½ cup onion, minced

⅛+ cup butter and ⅛+ cup olive oil, mixed

4 slices bread, cubed

⅓+ cup water, halved

¼ teaspoon dried tarragon

⅛ teaspoon coarse black pepper

½ pound shrimp, peeled, de-veined, cooked, and chopped

½ teaspoon salt or a little less

½ cup tomato juice

2 teaspoons cornstarch

2 tablespoons grated, low-fat Romano cheese

Combine fish and ¼+ cup of lime juice in a 13 × 9 × 2 baking dish. Cover and let stand for a half hour.

Sauté onion in butter/oil mixture in a generous skillet until tender. Add bread cubes, tossing lightly. Stir in ⅓ cup water, tarragon, and pepper before removing from heat. Add the remaining lime juice, the minced cooked shrimp, and salt. Stir thoroughly and set aside.

Remove the mullet from the lime juice; drain the fish and discard the juice. Return three mullet fillets to the baking dish and spread the shrimp mixture over them. Top with the other three fillets. Pour tomato juice around the fillets, cover the dish with aluminum foil and bake at 350° F for about 30 minutes. Carefully remove the foil and bake the fish for an additional 10 minutes or until it passes the easy-flake test. Drain the cooking liquid from the fish into a small pan, leaving mullet and stuffing mixture in dish. Combine cornstarch and remaining water, stirring to remove lumps. Stir this sauce into leftover cooking liquid and bring to a boil. Cut the heat down and simmer for 2 minutes or until thickened. Remove from heat. Pour sauce over fish, sprinkle with cheese, and broil four inches from heating element about 3 minutes or until browned. Cut stuffed fish into serving portions and serve immediately to up to six persons. We'll be looking for your cards and letters on this one.

Mullet Festival Special

Feel festive? Try this one.

2 pounds mullet fillets, fresh or frozen

½ cup rich French dressing

1-½ cups crushed cheese crackers (We recommend Castle Crest brand reduced-fat cheddar crackers.)

2 tablespoons peanut oil

Paprika

Thaw fish if frozen. Carefully skin fillets and cut into serving-sized portions. Dip each fillet in dressing and roll in cracker crumbs. Place on a well-greased cookie sheet, approximately 15 × 12, and drizzle oil over the mullet. Sprinkle with paprika. Bake in a very hot (500°) oven for 10 to 13 minutes or until fillets flake easily when fork tested. Should serve up to six persons.

Mullet Apple Turbans

Thank the state of Florida's seafood kitchens for the framework from which we adapted this great, healthy recipe!

2 pounds mullet fillets (boneless preferred)

1-½ teaspoon salt

¼ teaspoon pepper

1-½ cups tart apples, peeled and grated

1 10-¾-ounce can chicken broth

1 6-ounce package onion-garlic croutons

2 eggs, beaten well

¼ cup chopped parsley

3 tablespoons dry white wine

1 tablespoon butter and *1 tablespoon olive oil, mixed*

Use a little of the butter/oil mixture to grease an 8 × 8 × 2 baking dish. Cut fillets into serving-sized portions and sprinkle with one teaspoon of the salt and the pepper. Roll fillets turban style, skin side in, and secure with a wooden pick. Stand turbans on end in the greased baking dish. In a large bowl, combine apple, chicken broth, croutons, eggs, parsley, and remaining ½ teaspoon salt. Spoon stuffing equally into center of each turban. Combine wine with remaining oil mixture and brush stuffed turbans with it. Bake at 350° F, basting occasionally, for 25 to 30 minutes or until the fish passes fork test. Should serve six.

Black Baked Mullet

A remarkable demonstration of black magic

4 mullet fillets, about ¼ pound each

Nonstick low-fat cooking oil spray

¼ cup cornmeal

1 teaspoon dried thyme

1 teaspoon dried basil

½ teaspoon garlic powder

½ teaspoon lemon pepper

4 teaspoons blackening seasoning

½ teaspoon paprika

Coat a baking sheet thickly with the cooking oil spray. Combine cornmeal, thyme, and basil on a large plate, mixing well. Sprinkle ⅛ teaspoon of garlic powder, ⅛ teaspoon of lemon pepper, and a teaspoon of the blackening seasoning on each of the fillets. Then coat each fillet with the cornmeal mixture and put them in the prepared baking pan. Dust each fillet with ⅛ teaspoon of paprika and coat lightly with oil spray. Put baking sheet on the bottom shelf of oven and bake for 20 minutes, then reduce to 350° F and bake for an additional five minutes, or until the crust is golden. The fish is done when the fillets flake easily. Serves two to four.

Great Southern Savory Baked Mullet

One of the most popular, basic, and tasty of baked mullet recipes is this one, traditionally calling for six strips of bacon. Feel free to substitute soy bacon or experiment with imitation bacon crumbles such as are often used on salads, but don't use too many.

2 pounds mullet fillets

2 teaspoons lemon juice

Black pepper

6 slices of bacon or bacon substitute

1 cup thinly sliced onion

½ cup soft bread crumbs

2 tablespoons chopped parsley

For best results, skin fillets. Place fillets in a single layer in a 12 × 8 × 2 baking dish coated with cooking oil spray. Sprinkle with lemon juice and pepper. Fry bacon until crisp, remove from pan, let cool on absorbent paper, and then crumble. Sauté onion until tender. Remove onion from pan and arrange evenly over fillets. Combine bacon, bread crumbs, and parsley. Sprinkle mixture over fillets. Bake in a 350° F oven for 25 to 30 minutes or until fish passes fork test. Serves six to eight.

Foiled Mullet

1-½ cups fresh mushrooms, sliced
½ cup onions, chopped
1 tablespoon olive oil
1 cup tomatoes, chopped
2 tablespoons dry white wine
½ teaspoon dried, crushed thyme,
⅛ teaspoon black pepper
1 pound mullet in 4-ounce fillets

For best results, skin fillets. In a large skillet, sauté mushrooms and onions in oil. Add all ingredients except fish. Cut a piece of foil twice the length of a baking pan. Place in pan and spray with a cooking oil spray. Arrange fish in a single layer on the foil and top with vegetable mixture. Bring foil up over fish, closing all edges. Bake at 350° F for 10 to 15 minutes or until the fish flakes readily when forked. Serve to four hungry people.

Mullet with Coral Sauce

Named neither for Cape Coral nor the reefs of the Florida
Keys but for the coral color of this baked mullet's topping, here's another recipe based on one from the state of
Florida's Department of Environmental Protection,
where mullet promotion is an official mission.

2 pounds mullet fillets, skin on

⅛ cup butter and ⅛ cup peanut or olive oil, mixed

2 tablespoons lemon juice

1 teaspoon grated onion

1 teaspoon paprika

1 teaspoon salt

⅛ teaspoon red pepper

Arrange fillets skin down in 12 × 8 × 2 oiled baking
dish. Combine remaining ingredients in a bowl and mix
well. Pour sauce over fish and bake at 350° F for 20 to 25
minutes or until the fish flakes easily when tested with a
fork. Should provide six mouth-watering servings.

Crunchy Creme Mullet

The recipe is amazing, the results sure to astound your
palate.

1 pound fresh, skinless mullet fillets

½ teaspoon salt

½ cup low-fat sour cream

½ cup mayonnaise (low-fat OK)

*½ package (½ ounce or less) of ranch-style salad
    dressing*

*3 ounces garlic-, onion-, or chive-flavored low-fat
    crackers, crumbled*

Cut fillets into serving-sized portions and sprinkle
lightly with salt. Combine sour cream, mayo and salad
dressing mix, stirring until thoroughly homogenized.
Place this salad dressing in a shallow dish and dip the
fish pieces into it and then into a pan containing the
cracker crumbs. Place fish portions on a 15 × 9 × 1
baking pan coated with cooking oil spray and bake for 20
or so minutes at 350° F, until the fish flakes readily when
forked. Should serve five or six and bring smiles to all.

Broccolotti Mullet

This recipe is supplied for the one-in-a-thousand person who really isn't crazy about the distinct mullet flavor. If you know someone like that, give 'em this recipe with assurances they'll love it. (Unless they happen to be one of those rare persons—like a recent U.S. President—who don't, heaven forbid, like broccoli!)

2 pounds mullet fillets (boned, skin on)

2 tablespoons lemon juice

2 tablespoons fresh or instant minced onion

1 package (10 ounces) frozen chopped broccoli

1 package (½ ounce or more) Italian salad dressing

1 tablespoon grated low-fat Parmesan cheese

1 jar (2 ounces) sliced pimentos, drained

Thaw fish if frozen. Place fish in a single layer, skin side down, in a 12 × 8 × 2 baking dish coated with cooking oil spray. Brush the mullet with lemon juice. In a separate sauce pan add onion to broccoli and cook according to package directions. Arrange cooked broccoli over fish. Combine salad dressing mix and Parmesan cheese, sprinkle it over the broccoli, and top with pimento slices. (Pretty!) Now bake at 350° F for 25 to 30 minutes or until the fish flakes readily when tested with a fork. Feeds five or six.

Mullet, for complicated reasons, does not "keep" as well as most fish and even when flash frozen is suspect after twelve days. Heavily iced in the round, mullet are good for up to thirty hours. Fresh fillets surrounded by ice should be discarded after sixteen hours. They may not be spoiled but there will be a significant deterioration of flavor quality with every passing minute.

The Mysterious, Magical Mullet Loaf

Builds bodies sixteen ways, probably more! Get set for an adventure in baking and eating.

1 pound skinned, boned mullet fillets

1 cup boiling water

1 sweet onion, sliced

2 tablespoons lemon juice

½ teaspoon salt

1 loaf Vienna or French bread, about 14 inches long

1 cup shredded low-fat cheddar cheese

½ cup low-fat salad dressing such as Miracle Whip

½ cup chili sauce

½ cup chopped dill pickles

¼ cup sliced green onions

1 tablespoon horseradish

¼ teaspoon salt

Place fillets in a 10-inch fry pan. Add water, onion slice, lemon juice, and ½ teaspoon salt. Cover and simmer 5 to 10 minutes or until fish flakes when forked. Remove fish from liquid, drain, and chill. When thoroughly chilled, flake.

Cut the loaf of bread in half lengthwise and hollow out the top and bottom halves, leaving an outside shell ¾-inch thick. Tear the bread you removed from the center of the loaf into small pieces. Combine remaining ingredients, flaked fish, and bread pieces, mixing thoroughly. Pile all into bottom shell and mound up. Place top shell over filling. Wrap loaf securely in aluminum foil. Bake in a 400° F oven 40 minutes or until loaf is hot. Cut into thick chunks or slices. Serves five or six.

Lemon-Rice Stuffed Lisa

This was one of the earlier mullet recipes released by the state of Florida, possibly as far back as the 1950s when they were creatively but unsuccessfully marketing mullet under its Spanish name *Lisa.*

3 dressed mullet, 1-¼ to 1-½ pounds each

1-½ teaspoons salt

Lemon-Rice Stuffing (recipe follows)

2 tablespoons canola oil

Clean, wash, and dry fish. Sprinkle inside and out with salt. Stuff fish loosely. Close openings with small skewers or wooden picks. Place fish on well-greased baking pan. Brush with oil. Bake in 350° F oven, basting occasionally with cooking oil, for 30 to 35 minutes or until fish passes the fork test with ease. Remove skewers after it cools a little. Enough for six or seven people.

Lemon-Rice Stuffing

1 cup thinly sliced celery

½ cup finely chopped onion

3 tablespoons canola or safflower oil

1 can (4 ounces) sliced mushrooms, drained

2 cups cooked long grain and wild rice mix

2 tablespoons lemon juice

1 teaspoon grated lemon rind

½ teaspoon salt

*½ teaspoon fines herbes blend or ½ teaspoon minced
    parsley and ⅛ teaspoon rosemary*

Cook celery and onion in a little oil until celery is tender, then add mushrooms and continue heating. In a few moments, combine all ingredients and mix. Makes about 2-½ cups of exquisite stuffing.

Microcooked

Using a microwave oven, you can cook mullet in a number of different ways for an excellent variety of tasty presentations. Don't knock it till you've tried it. And who knows what to call it? Microwaving? Microcooking? Microwave cooking? Microbaking? We have opted for *Microcooking* since the process seems a little more like nuclear "cooking" than baking, although the finished product often does *resemble* conventionally baked fish. Still, there are significant differences, and we do invite and encourage mullet fans to seriously try microcooking and to experiment with their ovens and different recipes, ours and ad-libbed ones, to discover which combinations work best. And remember: Microcooking is one of the healthiest ways to cook almost anything, retaining most of the natural vitamins, minerals, oils and juices.

Quick Delish Fish

Use a whole scaled mullet of about a pound, dressed, with head off and fins removed.

Marinate it in garlic and lemon juice (or unsweetened lemonade) mixture for 30 minutes refrigerated. Then wrap the fish in plastic wrap and microcook on full power until cooked through, about 4 to 5 minutes depending on wattage. Two fish will take nearly double the time.

Chee-Zee Mullet

This recipe turns out mullet that has much of the "fresh fried" taste that traditional mullet fans overtly prefer. Yet, it's definitely un-fried and very un-fat. This was one of our earliest microwave successes at our kitchen deep in the woods of Dixie.

> *4 small to medium mullet, filleted virtually boneless, skins left on*
>
> *Olive oil*
>
> *Lime juice*
>
> *Jane's Krazy Mixed Up Pepper*
>
> *Garlic Salt*
>
> *Crushed cheese crackers (We recommend Castle Crest brand reduced-fat cheese crackers.)*

Cover the bottom of a shallow pan with oil, then add about the same amount of lime juice, fresh or packaged. Roll the fillets in the liquid and let them marinate for 15 to 30 minutes, refrigerated. Then remove from pan, shake dry and sprinkle liberally with both Jane's and garlic salt. Then roll in well-crushed cheese crackers. Place the seasoned fillets in a microwave baking dish and sprinkle additional crushed crackers on top of each. Microcook on high until the fish passes the flake test with a fork. Serve with pride and catch the smiles. If you want to move the taste slightly closer to the Mediterranean, add a little oregano to the marinade. Serves four.

Panhandled Almond Mullet

Here's how they do it in Pensacola.

> *1 pound of boneless mullet fillets*
>
> *¼ cup canola or olive oil*
>
> *½ cup slivered almonds*
>
> *½ teaspoon salt*
>
> *½ teaspoon white pepper*
>
> *2 teaspoons chopped parsley*
>
> *1 tablespoon lemon juice*

DEFROSTING FISH IN THE MICROWAVE

Bear in mind that microcooking is one of the most versatile cooking methods ever invented and experimentation is the key to culinary adventure. At the same time, there are certain general rules to be obeyed when microcooking, and here are some of those that apply specifically to seafood:

Frozen fish can be defrosted safely and without damage to the fish texture or quality by using a microwave oven's defrost settings and following these guidelines:

FILLETS: For 1 pound, defrost for 5-½ to 8 minutes, let stand for 10 minutes, then cook.

STEAKS: For 1 pound, defrost for 6 to 8 minutes, let stand for 15 minutes, then cook.

WHOLE: For a 1 to 1-½ pound whole cleaned mullet, defrost for 8 to 10 minutes, let stand for 15 minutes, then cook.

Half-way through the defrost cycle, turn the fish over. Fish should feel icy but pliable when proper defrosting is completed. The fish should be set aside for the specified period of time before it is rinsed, patted dry, and further prepared and cooked.

The fillets should be about 3 or 4 ounces each. Bring a little oil to cooking temperature (about a minute on high depending on the oven's wattage) in a micro-safe dish and then add the almonds, stirring them into the oil. Cook almonds in oil for about two minutes, then stir again. Remove the almonds and set aside. They will stay quite hot. Arrange the mullet fillets in a shallow baking dish with thinnest parts toward the center. Pour oil over the fillets; season with salt, pepper, parsley, and lemon juice. Cover the dish with slightly vented plastic wrap and cook on high for 2 minutes, after which the dish should be turned 180 degrees and the fish then cooked for another 2 minutes at 90 percent power. If your microwave oven has a carousel feature, there is, of course, no reason to turn the dish. Simply cook on high for 4 minutes or until the mullet passes the famous fork test. Garnish with the almonds, recover, and let stand three minutes before serving to two, three or four ready trial participants. This is one recipe all will be glad they tried!

Mullet Italiano

Here's a recipe straight from the number-one Italian seafood restaurant in the South (but we aren't naming any names).

4 boneless mullet fillets, 3 to 4 ounces each

2 tablespoons water

½ of a standard 10-ounce can of diced tomatoes with cut green chilies

1 jar (2-½ ounces) sliced mushrooms, drained

1 teaspoon cornstarch

½ teaspoon sugar

¼ teaspoon dried crushed basil

2 tablespoons shredded low-fat mozzarella cheese

Place fillets in a shallow baking dish, sprinkling the fish with water. Cover with clear plastic wrap; vent by leaving a small edge of the dish unsealed. Microcook on high for 6 to 9 minutes or until the fillets flake easily when tested with a fork. Remove fish and set aside while you prepare the sauce.

In a two-cup measure stir together the tomatoes and chilies, mushrooms, cornstarch, sugar, and basil. Microcook on high uncovered for 2 or 3 minutes or until it is thickened and bubbling. Stir every 40 seconds.

Now drain the fish completely, transfer to a micro-friendly serving platter, and pour the sauce over the fish. Sprinkle with cheese and then microcook uncovered on high for 30 to 60 seconds or until the cheese has melted. This recipe should produce enough fish for four mullet maniacs.

Lemon-Buttered Mullet

As you have correctly assumed, lemon goes well with mullet almost no matter how you use it—in a marinade, as a garnish, a sauce, a flavor-enhancer in stuffing, or as the final splash of variance such as is the case with this recipe. This one was sent to us by a famous chef now happily retired in Apalachicola, where mullet practically jump through his front window.

MICROCOOKING TIMES

Microwave cooking times vary greatly, depending on the make, design, and wattage of the particular oven being used.

There is a microwave-safe plastic dish generically known as the Fish Cooker that cooks fish very well at these timings in 600- to 700-watt ovens:

1 pound of fish fillets, ¼ inch thick—3 to 7 minutes

1 pound of fish fillets, ½ inch thick—4 to 8 minutes

1 pound of fish steaks, ¾ inch to 1 inch thick—6 to 8 minutes

1 to 1-½ pounds whole cleaned fish—8 to 10 minutes, then let stand 5 minutes before serving

Microwave ovens supply more cooking power at the outside edges of the central cooking area. Because of this, the thinner ends or sections of a fish should be folded under or aimed toward the center of the cooker so they don't overcook. Any fish being cooked in the microwave can be reliably checked at any point with the old-fashioned fork test. If the fish flakes easily and is opaque, it's done.

4 mullet fillets, skin on, bones in, about 4 ounces each

2 tablespoons real butter (with more butter to come)

1 tablespoon canola oil

Black pepper to taste

¼ cup (or more) real butter

2 tablespoons Florida lemon juice

2 tablespoons chopped fresh parsley

Preheat a micro browning dish, about 7 or 8 minutes on high. Add the 2 tablespoons of butter and the oil and keep heating for another 30 seconds; then sear the fillets and sprinkle with pepper. Microcook for 4 minutes or so or until the mullet flakes readily when fork tested. Cover and set aside. Make a lemon-butter sauce by melting the quarter cup of butter on high for 60 to 90 seconds. Add the lemon juice and chopped parsley, mixing well. This sauce is to be poured over the fillets as they are served. Serves two to four.

Note: Microwave browning dishes are not easy to find; one source is the Walter Drake mail order catalog.

Sweet & Sour Mullet

This is not your everyday down-South mullet recipe. No'sir, *sweet and sour* is not in the Old Dixie vocabulary, but here it is in a deep South mullet cookbook only because the contrasting taste sensations do work well with mullet's distinctive taste. Don't back away until you have put the following recipe (smuggled in from Singapore) to the test.

> *2 pounds diced celery*
>
> *1 clove garlic, crushed*
>
> *2 tablespoons all-purpose flour*
>
> *½ tablespoon non-iodized salt*
>
> *2 tablespoons brown sugar*
>
> *½ teaspoon black pepper*
>
> *¼ cup water*
>
> *¼ cup rice vinegar*
>
> *2 tablespoons chopped parsley*
>
> *½ teaspoon dill (optional)*

Preheat a microwave browning dish up to 8 minutes on high; add oil and heat on high an additional 20 to 30 seconds, searing the mullet fillets on both sides. Remove and set to one side. Reheat the dish; mix and sear the onions, garlic, and celery. Cook the 3-item veggie mixture for 1-½ to 2 minutes on high. Sprinkle mixture with flour and mix thoroughly, adding sugar, salt, pepper, water and vinegar. Keep mixing until virtually homogenized. Cover and cook for 3-½ to 6 minutes on high, stirring occasionally until the sauce is thick. Add parsley and dill. With care and caution, introduce the mullet to the sauce and continue cooking 2 to 4 minutes or until the fish passes the done test. All times and settings are adjustable to individual micro ovens. Serves six.

 Like chickens (and unlike most fish) mullet possess gizzards which, fried, some people prize.

Broiled

With all the emphasis on healthy cooking these days, the broiling of seafood has become more popular. The truth is, many of us mulletheads had discovered the delicious results of broiling even before health concerns brought the method into the public eye. What we found was that there is simply no better, no *tastier* way to prepare a fresh mullet than to broil it in a conventional oven or wherever you can control the heat above the fish. The broiling process is healthy because it is low-low-fat. The small amount of oil that may be used to baste the fish is virtually insignificant, and most of it dissipates during the cooking.

Here are a few of our favorite broiling recipes, plus some contributed by reliable mullet connoisseurs.

Valdosta Broiled Mullet Fillets

2 pounds fresh skinless mullet fillets

1 teaspoon salt

⅛ teaspoon pepper

¼ cup lime juice (fresh preferred)

3 tablespoons olive oil

Paprika

Lime wedges (as a garnish)

Cut the mullet into serving-sized portions of about 3 ounces each. Place these in a single layer in a shallow dish, sprinkling with salt and pepper. Pour lime juice over the fish and refrigerate for 30 minutes, turning once. Remove the fish from the juice and set the juice aside. Place fish on a broiler pan with a nonstick surface or coated with cooking oil spray. Combine the oil and the remaining lime juice; brush fish with the mixture and sprinkle with paprika. The fish should be broiled about 4 inches from the source of heat for 8 to 10 minutes or until it flakes easily when tested with a fork. Garnish with lime wedges. This recipe feeds six. Everybody will love it.

Citrus Sally's Lemon-Lime Mullet Broil

4 small- to medium-sized mullet, gutted but fins and head can be left on or removed

2 oranges

Juice of 1 lemon

3 tablespoons canola or olive oil

Pinch of each: salt, sugar, black pepper

Cut three slits in the sides of each fish; brush both sides with oil and sprinkle liberally with lemon juice, pepper, salt, and sugar. Position them in a nonstick broiler pan; slice the oranges and place the slices both under and on top of the fish. Broil for 3 to 5 minutes per side. Try to keep the orange pieces with the fish. Test with a fork. Serve with the "burnt" orange slices intact. When correctly cooked, the mullet meat will separate from the bones quite readily, making the eating process a lot more fun. The citrus influence in this recipe suits mullet to a T and will greatly please four diners.

Mayo-Lemon-Basil Mullet

Here's another citrus-enhanced broiling recipe, and this one is truly unusual, offering a medley of flavors.

1-½ to 2 pounds skinned mullet fillets

3 tablespoons low-fat mayonnaise

1 tablespoon lemon juice

1 teaspoon dried basil leaves

½ teaspoon onion powder

Nonstick cooking oil spray

Preheat the broiler. Using a whisk, combine the mayo, lemon juice, basil, and onion powder in a small mixing bowl. Mix well and set aside. The fish, cut to serving-sized portions of 3 to 4 ounces each, should be placed on a nonstick broiler pan. The top side of the fish should be as dry as possible; use paper towel. Spread each fillet with the mayo mix; using about half of it. Broil 6 to 8 inches from the heat for 5 to 6 minutes. Keep a sharp eye out for the topping's tendency to burn. Remove the fish, turn them, and coat the new up-sides with the remaining sauce. Broil for another 3 to 6 minutes or until the fish pass the fork test. Serves four to six.

Mayport Broil

Delicious and fast!

2 pounds mullet fillets

2 tablespoons canola or olive oil

2 tablespoons soy sauce

2 tablespoons Worcestershire sauce

1 teaspoon paprika

½ teaspoon chili powder

½ teaspoon garlic powder (not garlic salt!)

A dash of liquid hot pepper sauce

Lemon wedges

Place fillets in a single layer, skin side down, on a nonstick or sprayed broil-and-serve platter about 10 × 16 inches. Combine remaining ingredients except the lemon. Pour this sauce over the fillets and broil about 4 inches from the heat for 8 to 15 minutes or until the fish flakes easily when fork tested. Baste once during broiling with sauce in the pan. Serve with lemon wedges. Feeds five or six.

Broiled Lisa

Using the popular Spanish name for mullet is appropriate with this recipe which admittedly takes a little more than average preparation time. After all, it's very Latin to avoid any hurry, take your time, enjoy the fruits of patience.

About 2 pounds of whole mullet, cleaned, scaled, drawn (one, two, three fish)

Bay leaves

Sea salt and black pepper

Olive oil

Juice of one lemon

Wash the mullet thoroughly and sprinkle the gutted, de-blacked cavities with salt and pepper and insert a bay leaf. Brush the skin with olive oil and sprinkle with fresh lemon juice. Place under a preheated broiler and cook for 3 to 5 minutes before turning and then another 2 to 4 minutes or until done. Baste occasionally with lemon juice and olive oil while broiling. Test with a fork. Serve with the prepared spicy almond sauce below. When your friends ask where you found such a recipe, tell them about this book. Serves two to four.

Immokalmond Sauce

½ can (5 ounces) diced tomatoes and green chilies (We recommend Ro-Tel brand.)

3 tablespoons ground almonds (Grind in a coffee grinder if necessary.)

½ clove garlic, crushed

¼ teaspoon cayenne pepper

Pinch of sea salt

3 tablespoons red wine vinegar

½ cup olive oil

Mix all the sauce ingredients except oil and vinegar together until a paste consistency is achieved. Whisk in vinegar and oil gradually with vigorous stirring. Sauce may be stored a few minutes or a few days if placed in a tight container and refrigerated.

Smoky Broiled Mullet

Thank the state of Florida's official seafood kitchens for this creative recipe which mimics the taste of smoked mullet (see page 66), but offers a juicier, mellower fish than typically produced through traditional smoking. The recipe is slightly modified for good health.

2 pounds skinned mullet fillets, fresh preferred

⅓ cup reduced-sodium soy sauce

3 tablespoons olive or canola oil

1 tablespoon liquid smoke

1 clove garlic, minced

½ teaspoon ginger

¼ teaspoon salt

Lemon wedges as garnish

Cut the mullet into serving-sized portions of 3 to 4 ounces each. Combine the remaining ingredients (except the lemon) and mix thoroughly to create sauce. Place fish on a nonstick or sprayed broiler pan and brush with the sauce. Broil rather close—about 3 inches from the heat—7 to 12 minutes, turning once carefully and saucing the other side. Baste occasionally as necessary with any remaining sauce. When the fish flakes easily with a fork, it's ready. Serve with the lemon wedges to six soon-to-be-very-happy souls.

The state's official recipe points out that since mullet vary greatly in size from season to season, it can happen that any year's "run" of mullet yields fish too small to produce good fillets. Should this be the case, pan-dressed (scaled, gutted, heads off, fins on or off) mullet can be substituted and the same recipe used to bake the fish in a 13-½ × 8-¾ × 1-¾-inch baking dish sprayed with nonstick cooking oil spray. Pour sauce over fish and bake in a 350° F oven for 15 to 20 minutes or until the mullet flakes easily when forked. The fish should be basted three times during cooking.

Indian River Mullet Broil

Citrus flavoring returns front and center for this broiler recipe, which specifies one or two fresh-picked Indian River oranges, the juice of which is item number one on our list.

> *3 tablespoons Indian River orange juice mixed with 1 tablespoon canola or extra virgin olive oil*
>
> *Juice of 1 freshly squeezed lime*
>
> *1 tablespoon and another 2 teaspoons of reduced-sodium soy sauce*
>
> *2 teaspoons grated Indian River orange peel*
>
> *1 minced garlic clove*
>
> *½ teaspoon grated fresh ginger*
>
> *Nonstick cooking oil spray*
>
> *1 to 1-½ pounds of skin-on mullet fillets*

The marinade is essential to this project's success. Use a small bowl to combine the orange juice and oil mixture with the lime juice, soy sauce, orange rind, garlic, and ginger. Pour the sauce into a shallow oven-safe glass cooking dish large enough for the fillets. Place the fish in the dish and spoon some of the sauce over the pieces. Put in the fridge for 45 to 90 minutes. Put the marinated fish on a preheated broiler pan coated with nonstick cooking oil spray. Broil 5 to 6 inches from the heat for 7 to 9 minutes or until the fish just starts to flirt with black. Avoid burning. Baste once or twice while broiling. When blackening is plainly detected, shut down the heat and leave the fish in for another 3 to 5 minutes or until done. You have a low-fat dish loaded with flavor and nutrition.

 Striped mullet may be distinguished from closely related white mullet by counting their anal rays, which are eight and nine respectively.

Mrs. Dash's Mullet Almandine

This prize-winning recipe will feed six mullet gourmets so well they'll want to know when you're making it again.

> *2 pounds mullet fillets, cut into serving-sized pieces*
>
> *¼ cup all-purpose flour*
>
> *1-½ teaspoon Mrs. Dash's Original Seasoning*
>
> *½ teaspoon paprika*
>
> *¼ cup canola or olive oil*
>
> *½ cup sliced almonds*
>
> *2 tablespoons lemon juice*
>
> *5 drops any hot sauce made in New Iberia, Louisiana (There are no bad sauces made in this famous pepper town.)*
>
> *1 tablespoon chopped fresh parsley*
>
> *Parsley sprigs to be used as garnish*

Combine flour, Mrs. Dash, and paprika, and mix well. Dredge fish in flour mixture till thoroughly coated. Place the fish chunks in a 15 × 10 × 1 inch pan coated with nonstick cooking oil spray. Brush a few teaspoons of the oil over the fish and broil 4 inches from heat for 9 or 10 minutes or until the fish flakes when forked. Transfer to a serving platter; set aside and keep warm. Serves five or six.

Sauté the almonds in remaining oil in a small skillet until golden brown. Remove from heat and stir in remaining ingredients (except the parsley sprigs which are to be used as a garnish). Pour the almond sauce over the fish and serve.

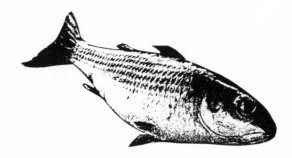

Muscadine Mullet

This unusual recipe calls for Great Southern Muscadine wine such as may be found in Georgia, Alabama, and Florida, but any good regional, fruity wine may be substituted.

4 small- to medium-sized dressed mullet, skins on

6 tablespoons low-sodium soy sauce

8 tablespoons muscadine wine

3 tablespoons sugar

3 tablespoons finely grated ginger

To marry Tallahassee and Tokyo, mix the soy sauce, six tablespoons of wine, sugar, and ginger over medium heat, stirring regularly. Bring barely to a boil and strain the results through a sieve. Combine 2 tablespoons of the sauce with the remaining wine and rub in the cavities and on the outsides of the fish. Place the remaining sauce back in the saucepan and bring to a boil, then reduce the heat so it can simmer until its volume has been quite reduced. Place fish on a pre-heated, stick-proofed broiler pan. Cook about 2 inches from the source of heat for 4 to 5 minutes or until fish flakes easily when tested; brush with the remaining reduced sauce and serve with pride. Enough for four.

Tamarind-Sesame Mullet BBQ

Another recipe of exotic character, this one introduces the delicate relationship of flavors represented by the mullet, the sesame and the tamarind. Tamarind juice (or nectar) is available at many larger food markets and virtually all Hispanic specialty markets.

1-½ pounds mullet fillets or steaks

⅓ cup tamarind nectar

3 tablespoons ketchup

1 tablespoon low-sodium soy sauce

2 tablespoons apple cider vinegar

1 tablespoon sesame oil

2 tablespoons dark brown sugar or (preferably) turbinado

Nonstick cooking oil spray

Toasted sesame seeds (optional)

Mix together the tamarind juice, ketchup, soy sauce, vinegar, sesame oil, and sugar. Pour over the mullet and marinate in the refrigerator for at least 2 hours, turning occasionally and basting. Then, preheat the broiler and coat the broiler pan with nonstick spray. Broil the fish 5 to 6 inches from heat for 3-½ to 5 minutes per side, basting the fish occasionally. If you have toasted sesame seeds available, sprinkle them on the fish pieces as served. By our calculations, this healthy mullet presentation delivers a mere 6 grams of fat per serving. Serves four or five.

 About three-fourths of all U.S. commercial mullet is from Florida. Mullet from Terra Ceia, Panacea, Charlotte Harbor, Steinhatchee, and Cedar Key is rated very highly by both locals and visiting mullet heads.

Grilled

While grilling mullet usually produces a product similar to the one achieved by broiling, there are several important differences. Grilling probably offers slightly more control over the process since the cook or chef is more personally involved and continually monitors the progress of the cooking. An outdoor gas grill can deliver turned-to-perfection mullet that is hard to match using any other method. I defended the charcoal grill for decades before I finally tried the LP route. And I found out: Gas is great! It offers fantastic control; you can adjust the heat with something that approaches precision. By using long-handled wire grilling baskets, you can turn the fish as necessary. Be sure, however, to coat such baskets with nonstick spray, or you may have difficulty removing the steaks or fillets from them. And, of course, don't turn the fish *too* often, or you'll tend to lose some of the moistness needed for consistency and flavor.

Perhaps the greatest overall advantage of grilling is the simple fact that it takes place outdoors, so most of the smoke and vapor is lost on the wind instead of becoming the pervading odor not only in the kitchen but most of the house. Furthermore, grilling is eminently healthy because most of the fat falls on the lava rocks or coals. If we don't ingest it, it can't clog our arteries.

And did I mention that grilled mullet is so delicious it defies description? It's true. If more people had tried grilling mullet, frying would not be the most popular method of mullet preparation. Have a mullet BBQ cookout and see if your guests don't urge you to have another such event as soon as possible!

As always, secure mullet as fresh as possible. For grilling purposes, gas or charcoal, larger fish with thicker fillets work best. While the grill (or basket) is still cold, coat it with nonstick spray or oil. Warm up a gas grill on high but lower the temperature to medium or low for cooking. Ample warm up of the lava rocks is essential for good results. When using charcoal, wait until a fine, white ash forms all over the hot coals. Cook your fish 2 to 3 inches or even a little higher above the flame. Don't overcook, but do try to "toast" the fish so its outside is slightly crisp. Baste the mullet with a prepared sauce or olive oil.

Fund raisers from churches to PTA groups in the South have traditionally used fish fries, often mullet, to draw the crowds. I can practically guarantee that our highly flavorful, grilled seafood will go over bigger and better than a conventional, high-fat fish fry! And the word will spread! Whether your event is a backyard, neighborhood get-together or an annual charity occasion designed to raise a bundle, this is the moment of history for grilled fish.

Grif's Dixie Broil

4 pounds fresh mullet fillets, skin on

⅓ cup extra virgin olive oil

1 teaspoon Cavender's Greek Seasoning

Remove the "black" lining from the belly section of the fillets. Brush the fillets with olive oil and place them in a shallow pan or pans in the fridge or on ice for 20 to 30 minutes before grilling. Put the oiled fillets skin side down in a cool, oiled hinged grilling cage or directly on a nonstick grill with flame or coals 2 to 4 inches below the fish. Generously sprinkle the top of each fillet with Cavender's Greek Seasoning and begin grilling. Baste with additional oil as necessary. Adjust height of flame or grill to avoid burning. Turn when skin starts to curl or crisp, usually 4 to 5 minutes or less. Brown seasoned side (about 2 or 3 minutes, tops) then turn again and test with a fork. If the mullet flakes easily, remove from grill and use a sharp, thin spatula to retrieve the barbecued fillets. Serve without delay. Fantastic fare with malt vinegar, barbecue sauce, or Dixie Red Sauce (page 21). Should serve a party of 6 to 10 people, who will mark their calendars should you plan on doing this again any-time soon.

INTERNATIONAL GRILLED MULLET

The outdoor chef's secret is to control the flavor with the marinade. Grilled mullet can reflect the Old South when the fish has been marinated in barbecue sauce or the Far East when the marinade is soy- or ginger-based, and the possibilities go on almost endlessly. Following are just a few of the best.

Creole Grilled Mullet

1-½ pounds mullet fillets, skin on

¼ cup tamari or soy sauce

2 tablespoons garlic powder

1 tablespoon water

2 tablespoons fresh lemon juice or wine vinegar

2 tablespoons creole seasoning (We recommend Tony's brand.)

Place the ingredients (except the mullet) in a large, re-sealable plastic food bag. Seal and shake like mad. Add the fish to the bag, reseal, and refrigerate for 90 minutes, turning the bag occasionally. Then, put the fillets in handled grilling baskets or on the grill, skin side down. If you're using wood or charcoal, add a few hickory wood chips (dry hickory nut shells will work also) for down-home smoke flavor. For gas grills, hickory smoke liquid seasoning may be sparingly applied to the fish. Baste occasionally with the leftover marinade. Turn at least once; test with a fork for doneness. Serve with lemonade on the rocks garnished with a sprig of mint. Enough for two to four persons.

 Most mullet gourmets rate mullet under two pounds as the best for flavor.

¡Si! ¡Si! Grilled Mullet

This spicy recipe calls for a pound of fillets with unscaled skin on. You read it right: skin and scales.

1 pound mullet fillets, unscaled skins on

Juice of 1 plump, ripe lime

1 teaspoon Worcestershire sauce (We recommend Lea & Perrins brand.)

About 2 ounces of extra virgin olive oil

1 teaspoon garlic powder

1 teaspoon cayenne pepper

Start by coating the fillets with a mixture of lime juice, garlic powder, Worcestershire sauce, and cayenne. Marinate for an hour, refrigerated. Coat the fillets with olive oil prior to grilling. Place skin side down and grill for 8 to 10 minutes or until fish starts turning opaque. Baste liberally with marinade, turn, and grill until deliciously browned. Do not overcook. Feeds two to four depending on appetites and occasion.

Mullet grow as large as twenty-three pounds (the world record, caught near Clearwater, Florida) but rarely top eight pounds. A typical catch is dominated by tops-in-taste one-to-three pounders.

Bubba's Barbecue Mullet

To do this one, you'll need several flavor enhancers.

1-½ *pounds fresh mullet fillets*

½ *cup ketchup*

¼ *cup olive oil*

3 tablespoons lemon juice

2 tablespoons apple vinegar

2 tablespoons hickory smoke seasoning

1 teaspoon Worcestershire sauce

1 teaspoon salt

½ *teaspoon grated onion*

½ *teaspoon dry mustard*

¼ *teaspoon paprika*

1 clove garlic, minced

3 drops liquid hot pepper sauce

Cut the mullet into serving-sized portions. Place in a single layer in baking pan, approximately 12 × 8 × 2 inches. Combine remaining ingredients to form a marinade which is to be poured over the fish. Marinate refrigerated for 15 minutes, turn and marinate 15 minutes longer. Remove the fillets but keep the remaining sauce for basting. Place fish in well-oiled, hinged wire grills, cooking about 4 inches from moderately hot coals (or rocks) for 5 or 6 minutes, basting with sauce. Turn and grill another 4 to 6 minutes or until the fish flakes easily when tested with a fork. Feeds four.

Barcelona BBQ

Featuring the genuine, *the original,* Barcelona Barbecue Sauce, whose recipe follows this one.

1-½ pounds skinned mullet fillets

¼ teaspoon sea salt

¼ teaspoon fresh coarsely ground black pepper

Orange slices (as a garnish)

Sprinkle the fillets with salt and pepper. Brush both sides of each fillet with Barcelona BBQ Sauce and place fillets in a nonstick hinged wire grill about 4 inches from flame or coals. Grill for up to 7 minutes, basting with sauce as needed. Turn and cook 4 to 6 minutes longer or until fish passes the flake test. Garnish with orange slices. Makes four servings.

Barcelona Barbecue Sauce

½ cup premium orange juice

⅓ cup ketchup

3 tablespoons brown sugar

2 tablespoons lemon juice

2 tablespoons minced, fresh onion

1 tablespoon soy sauce

Mix all ingredients thoroughly and use for brushing and basting.

The French Lieutenant's Mullet

Recommended for official occasions such as lunch on the governor's lawn.

1-½ pounds mullet fillets

½ cup olive oil

½ cup sesame seeds

⅓ cup cognac

⅓ cup fresh lemon juice

3 tablespoons low-salt soy sauce

½ teaspoon table salt

1 large clove garlic, crushed

Cut fillets into serving-sized portions and place in a single layer in a baking pan, approximately 12 × 8 × 2 inches. Combine remaining ingredients and pour the resulting sauce over the mullet, marinating for 30 minutes, refrigerated. Turn once. Place fish in nonstick, long-handled, shallow wire baskets. Grill about 4 inches above heat for 6 or 7 minutes. Baste, turn, and grill another 6 to 8 minutes or until the fork test is passed. Serves four.

Smoked

Smoked mullet rates as a delicacy, a Southern specialty of sensational character. There is nothing in the world even similar to smoked mullet. To emphasize this point allow me to refer to actual events in recent history.

With the gill net ban law of the mid-1990s in Florida, the price of mullet increased gradually but markedly until, in many markets, it was priced as high or higher than such premier fish as salmon and mahi-mahi. I once found smoked salmon, smoked mahi-mahi, and smoked mullet displayed together at the Winn-Dixie Marketplace near my home. Seeing that they were all at about the same price, I thought I might compare them. I did, and have since repeated the experiment. Neither mahi-mahi nor salmon can touch the unique, nutty mullet taste, so clean and so buttery and distinctive. Smoked mackerel is *nearly* as good, and smoked pompano is not something to pass over. But I repeat: In the smoked department, *nothing touches mullet.* It's as good as it gets.

If you are among the legions of people who have somehow missed the smoked mullet phenomenon, try to find the product somewhere. Many coastal roadside vendors and supermarkets have smoked mullet almost year-round but especially in early spring, the prime mullet season. Or better yet, acquire fresh mullet and do it yourself—as we'll get to in a moment. In the meantime, consider also a famous outdoor restaurant, Ted Peters in Pasadena (a suburb of St. Petersburg, Florida) where what is quite possibly the world's best smoked mullet is served whenever fresh mullet is available. Indeed, the Peters' elegantly rustic smoke house has been a seafood tradition for nearly fifty years in the Pinellas County hub of Florida and is famous world-wide for the excellence of its product. To taste Ted Peters' smoked mullet is to have a small idea of the essence of heaven. An exaggeration? Go to Pasadena, order the smoked mullet plate, and report back.

ST. PETERSBURG, FLORIDA

Let Ted Peters' smoked mullet be your inspiration as you cook. But don't expect to match its depth of flavor. You may, of course, set a whole new standard of your own where comparisons are irrelevant. Don't be afraid of failure. Over-smoking can be redeemed by calling the finished product Mullet Jerky. Remember that the wood and chips used are major contributors to final flavor. Sample, also, the smoked mullet featured in such Florida places as Cedar Key, Gibsonton, Bayport, Hudson, Punta Gorda, Pine Island, Chokoloskee, Newport, Eastpoint, Pensacola, Apalachicola, Panacea, Ft. Pierce, St. Augustine, and Fernandina.

Bear in mind that in some parts of Florida and elsewhere in the coastal South, mullet is primarily a bait species. (Strange but true.) And if you make an innocent local inquiry: "Does anyone around here smoke mullet?" you may be greeted by strange stares and grins. Still, it's worth asking the question because you may luck into something so good, so different, so tasty you will want to memorize it. Individual smoked mullet entrepreneurs in isolated areas show astounding innovation and a diversity as unique as they are themselves. We have come across local smokers that produce a mullet product so different in taste as to be quite indescribable, using unlikely combinations of bay leaves, fennel, cayenne, salsa, citrus, honey, hickory, and peppers in ways that don't make sense but make awfully good eatin' with a frosted mug of draft or a glass of blushed wine or even a Vernors or Schweppes. Smoked mullet demands a beverage of some kind, preferably on the tart or sharp side. Ginger ale is OK, ginger beer better, lemon or limeade is ideal. Medium dry wines or even Chianti are nice, too. So is champagne.

A charcoal or water smoker can be purchased at a department store or home specialty discount outlet for surprisingly little money. A good, affordable brand is Brinkmann's. Next find a source of hickory wood, red bay wood, and red bay leaves, and you will be well on your way to mullet smoking success.

Maximo Point Smoked Mullet

You can use a regular charcoal grill with a cover. Or there are special "smoker grills" that bring bragging results.

> *6 dressed mullet of medium size, butterfly cut or spinal split if possible*
>
> *3/4 cup salt*
>
> *1 package prepared crab boil*
>
> *1 gallon water*
>
> *1/4 cup olive oil*
>
> *1 pound hickory chips, soaked in 2 quarts of water overnight*

The traditional way of preparing the whole mullet is to remove the head just above where the collarbone would be if fish had collarbones and cut along the backbone almost to the tail so that the mullet lies flat in one piece. Wash the fish until clean. Add salt and crab boil to water and stir until dissolved. Pour this seasoned brine over the mullet and refrigerate for 30 minutes. Remove from brine and rinse in cold water; then dry.

If using a cooker designed specifically for smoking, follow its manufacturer's instructions for use. You may also wish to refer to the guidelines which follow when you're ready to innovate beyond the instruction booklet. If you're using a smoker with shelves and water pan, arrange the fish on the rack at lowest shelf in smoker. The water pan should be filled to about half full with leftover water from the hickory chips. Close the smoker's lid and open the vent slightly to keep smoke and air circulating. Estimated time is 1-½ to 2 hours.

If you are using charcoal or wood fire in a traditional barbecue grill with cover or hood, here are professional smokers' tips: Let the fire burn down to a low, glowing, even heat. Cover with wet (overnight-soaked, then drained and partially dried) hickory chips. The chips make the smoke. Place the fish on a well-oiled grill, skin side down, about 4 to 6 inches from the smoking coals. Baste fish well with oil at beginning and occasionally during cooking. Cover and smoke for 1-½ to 2 hours or until the mullet flakes easily when tested with a fork. Add remaining chips as needed to keep the fire smoking. Do *not* put the fire out with too many chips, and do *not* open the cooker too often, venting the smoke and heat. Small twigs of red bay and bay leaves added during the last 20 minutes of smoking will add pleasant flavoring. What we're describing here obviously is what well could be called a delicate balance!

If you're using mullet fillets instead of the traditional spinal cut, shorten the cooking time to 45 minutes, or even less if fish readily passes flake test. With smoking, however, a little over-cooking usually is better than undercooking.

Smoked mullet may be served on a platter with barbecue sauce, hot sauce, advanced tartar sauces (see Beyond Tartar, page 74) and other condiments. Osceola homemade Hot Sauce is one of the best. We also have found Trappey's store-bought BBQ sauce to be an outstanding sauce for mullet of all persuasions. And not only is smoked mullet one of the best of all seafood specialties, it is equally and uniquely spectacular at forming the essential "base" for a number of separate items such as spreads, salads, and sandwiches. Some tasty examples are offered up in this chapter.

Old Tampa Bay Smoked Mullet Spread

This stuff is so wonderful on crackers that some water-front cafes serve it not just as a freebie appetizer but as a featured specialty for a price and patrons are delighted.

1-½ pounds smoked mullet

1-¼ cups reduced-fat mayonnaise

2 tablespoons chopped parsley

2 tablespoons finely chopped sweet pickle

1 tablespoon prepared yellow salad mustard

2 teaspoons instant or fresh minced onion

2 teaspoons finely chopped celery

1 clove garlic, minced

1 dash Worcestershire sauce

Remove skin and bones from the smoked flesh. Flake fish well. Combine all ingredients. Mix well and chill for at least one hour before serving. Makes about 3-½ cups of spread. Serve with fresh, crisp, reduced-fat crackers. Expect compliments. This recipe is not patented. Pass it on.

 GOOD TO REMEMBER: One pound of smoked mullet equals about one and a half cups of flaked, smoked fish.

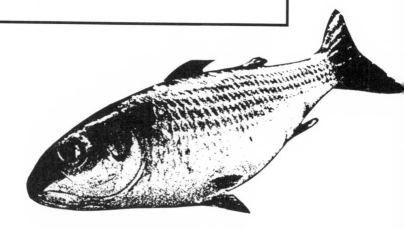

Arcadia Smoked Mullet Sandwich

Better known as a Mullet Western. The inventor of this recipe let mullet take over when ham didn't show. To put it plainly, a Western omelet becomes an improved product when smoked mullet is substituted for other meats. You will never see this item on the menu at Waffle House, but if it were offered, the Mullet Western undoubtedly would become so popular we would have to learn in a hurry how to successfully "aquaculture" mullet, making it as plentiful as pond-raised catfish. So, keep this recipe to yourself, or at least away from Waffle House's scouts, for the time being. The resource is not yet ready for that level of popularity.

¾ pound fresh smoked mullet

2 1-¼ ounce packages of Western-style omelet seasoning mix

1 cup water

10 eggs (For a heart-healthy recipe, remove the yolks from five of them.)

4 tablespoons olive or canola oil

12 slices wheat or bran bread (We recommend Arnold's Natural brand.)

4 tablespoons reduced-fat mayonnaise

Remove skin and bones from smoked mullet and flake the fish well. Combine seasoning mix with water. Add fish and eggs and beat until mixed well. In a 10-inch skillet heat enough oil to cover the bottom of the pan. Pour half of the omelet mixture into the skillet. As the mixture sets, lift edges with spatula or fork, allowing uncooked portion to run under cooked portion of omelet. When bottom of omelet is lightly browned and top is soft and creamy, fold sides over and slide from skillet onto plate. Cut omelet into thirds. Repeat procedure for remaining mixture. Spread slices of bread liberally with mayo and top with six slices of prepared omelet, cover with remaining six slices, and call them six Western sandwiches.

Judy's Mullet Butter

Contributed by seafood-savvy Judy Mastick of Suwannee, Florida

½ pound boned smoked mullet chunks

1 bunch green onions, chopped

1 teaspoon dill

1 teaspoon tarragon

1 garlic clove, smashed or chopped

Freshly ground black pepper

1 pint light sour cream

Juice of ½ a lemon

Mix ingredients together, garnish with black olives and lemon slices. Dip, spread, smile!

Emperor Mullet's Smoky Caesar Salad

Here is a sparkling treasure of a salad that should make the day of the six you serve.

1 cup smoked mullet, boned and torn into small pieces

3 tablespoons balsamic vinegar

½ cup olive oil

½ teaspoon garlic salt

Italian seasoning mix (optional)

1 egg

1 head romaine lettuce

2 cups low-fat Italian-style croutons

Juice of 1 small lemon

Fresh ground pepper

4 tablespoons grated low-fat Parmesan cheese

Boil the egg for one minute, then break it into a bowl and beat well with the lemon juice, garlic salt, and pepper. Combine the vinegar and olive oil and toss the lettuce and smoked mullet pieces with the dressing mixture. Then add the egg mixture. Add a dash or two of Italian seasoning if you wish. Toss enthusiastically to coat the salad thoroughly. Transfer to a new serving bowl and sprinkle the master salad with croutons and Parmesan cheese. Do not chill; serve at room temperature. Crumbled low-fat feta cheese may be substituted for Parmesan if you're feeling more Greek than Italian.

Keaton Beach Smoked Mullet Dinner Salad

½ pound fresh smoked mullet

1 cup reduced-fat mayonnaise or salad dressing such as Miracle Whip

1 teaspoon prepared brown mustard

½ teaspoon crushed tarragon leaves

½ teaspoon salt

¼ teaspoon celery seed

3 cups chilled, sliced, cooked potatoes

2 cups sliced celery

⅔ cup sliced radishes

⅓ cup sliced green onions

Lettuce leaves

The skin and bones should be removed from the mullet, and it should be flaked. Combine mayo, mustard, tarragon, salt, and celery seed; mix well. Fold in sliced potatoes. Cover and refrigerate for several hours to blend flavors. Add celery, radishes, onion, and flaked fish, mixing carefully. Arrange in center of lettuce-lined serving dish. Garnish with additional smoked mullet slices. Serves six.

 Translated into English, the scientific name for mullet basically means "bullet-headed" or "helmet-headed."

Beyond Tartar

A sauce to serve with smoked mullet

¾ cup low-fat mayonnaise

1 eggs

3 tablespoons fresh lemon juice

1 teaspoon sea salt

1 teaspoon prepared brown mustard

1 teaspoon sugar

1 teaspoon instant minced onion

2 drops liquid hot pepper sauce

Dash of black pepper

LOW-TEMP SMOKING

Back in the 1980s, Scientists W. Steven Otwell, John Koburger, and Robert Degner at the University of Florida were a principal part of a team of seafood researchers who, in search of ways to heighten mullet's marketability, developed a low-temperature smoking technique for the express purpose of preserving mullet's edibility and quality up to three months when frozen. Their findings are as important and applicable today as they were when first announced and publicized.

Here are the details: The fish should be skinned and filleted fresh, soaked for 30 minutes in four-percent brine and then dried for 30 minutes in refrigeration. The fish is then smoked for 90 minutes at a mere 120° F. An oven or broiler thermometer is essential, since a higher temperature will result in overcooked fish. After smoking, the fillets are allowed to cool and then are carefully packaged and frozen. They may also be used immediately by frying or otherwise completing the cooking process.

Low-temp smoked mullet fillets may be pan fried, deep fried, microcooked, broiled, or grilled. Their moisture content will be similar to regular fresh mullet because the smoking process was not hot enough to cause dehydration. So, handle the fillets the same as you would fresh fish. You can even batter them. By whatever method you finish them off, you can season them as you wish, be it on the light side or spicy barbecue.

¾ cup olive or canola oil

⅓ cup chopped parsley

1 tablespoon fresh horseradish

1 clove garlic, minced

In a blender, combine mayo, egg, lemon juice, salt, sugar, onion, mustard, liquid hot pepper sauce, and pepper. Cover; blend a few seconds. Uncover; add oil slowly, keeping motor running. Blend until thick and smooth. Add parsley, horseradish, and finally garlic; continue blending until very smooth. Serve with smoked mullet. Makes over 2 cups of Beyond Tartar.

ENTER THE SEA DOG

Because LTS (low-temp smoked) mullet is a skinless fillet and can be cut and shaped very easily to fit a sub-style or hot dog bun, LTS is an excellent way to prepare "sandwich mullet."

Our original Sea Dog Sandwich recipe calls for a long, slim LTS mullet fillet grilled or broiled and then dropped on a fresh, warm frank roll along with chopped onion, chopped tomato, ketchup, deli mustard, and lettuce. Ask for it by name: "One Sea Dog all the way— to go." And if your favorite seafood drive-in doesn't have it, make a Sea Dog of your own from the instructions above.

According to University of Florida consumer surveys of this product, preference panelists could not distinguish between low-temperature smoked mullet and either fresh fish or conventionally frozen fish when completely cooked. Panelists even gave high marks to low-temp fillets which had been stored frozen as long as ninety days. For mullet, that's an unbelievably long time. (Even with low-temp, *we* still say eat it ASAP.)

Lisa Dip

This recipe was smuggled in from Cuba.

½ pound smoked mullet

2 teaspoons lemon juice

Dash of ground cloves

½ teaspoon salt

6 peppercorns, crushed

1 cup low-fat sour cream

2 teaspoons chopped chives

1 teaspoon instant minced onion

¼ teaspoon dried rosemary (optional)

3 tablespoons chopped parsley

Remove skin and bones from the mullet and flake to very small pieces. Combine all ingredients except parsley. Chill for an hour or more. Sprinkle the dip with parsley and serve with crackers. Makes about 1-³/₄ cups of the original and internationally famous Lisa Dip.

Pasadena Pete's Hot German Potato Salad

This is a favored side dish for which we supply the following traditional recipe by Pasadena Pete, an old Pinellas Kraut to whom we express thanks for this classic culinary winner.

5 baking potatoes (Yellow gourmet potatoes are ideal.)

⅓ cup vinegar

1 teaspoon salt

1 teaspoon light brown sugar or turbinado

1 package lean bacon lightly fried and then chopped (easily scissored)

4 eggs (removing two yolks)

¾ cup chopped green onions or ½ cup chopped sweet onion

Boil potatoes until soft; peel and dice. Add vinegar, sugar, and salt. Lightly scramble the whites of four and yolks of two eggs for four minutes. Combine potatoes, bacon, leftover oil, soft-cooked eggs, and chopped onion. Mix well. Serve hot on a bed of lettuce with sizzling-hot smoked mullet. For most appetizing effect, serve on heat-holding metal platters if available. Serves six.

Osceola Hot Sauce

½ cup honey (palmetto if available)

½ cup prepared brown mustard

½ cup cider vinegar

¼ cup Worcestershire sauce

1 tablespoon chopped parsley

2 teaspoons liquid hot pepper sauce

1 teaspoon salt

Blend honey and mustard; stir in the remaining ingredients and heat to boiling. Serve with smoked mullet. Makes about 1-½ cups of a medium-hot, palate-tingling sauce.

Smoked Mullet Romanoff

A fish-and-noodle dish of unique, delightful flavors

1 pound smoked mullet, no skin or bones, flaked

1 8-ounce package egg noodles

2 cups large curd, low-fat cottage cheese

1-¼ cups low-fat sour cream

⅔ cup sliced whole green onions

2 cloves garlic, minced

2 teaspoons Worcestershire sauce

½ teaspoon liquid hot pepper sauce

¼ teaspoon pepper

½ cup grated Parmesan cheese

Flake the fish, removing any remaining small bones. Cook noodles according to package directions and drain well. Combine mullet, cooked noodles, cottage cheese, sour cream, onions, garlic, Worcestershire sauce, liquid hot pepper sauce, and pepper. Pour into a non-stick 2-quart shallow baking dish. Sprinkle Parmesan cheese over the top and bake in a moderate (350° F) oven for 20 to 25 minutes or until heated thoroughly. Enough for six grateful diners.

Finger mullet (young mullet) and cut mullet are among the best and favorite baits of big game sports fishers.

More Mullet

There are many ways to cook a mullet. There are ways that haven't even been invented yet! But here's a collection of fairly uncommon (but fantastic in results) cooking methods and how they apply for our celebrity fish, Mr. Mugil.

Molly O'Mullet Stew

Aye, and ye won't need a shamrock for good luck. Sup a steaming bowl of O'Mullet Stew and nothing but good will come to you.

1-½ to 2 pounds of skinless, boneless mullet fillets

1 cup sliced onions

1 cup sliced carrots

1 cup sliced leeks

¼ cup olive oil

2 cups chopped tomatoes

2 quarts clam juice

2 cups dry white wine

2 bay leaves

½ teaspoon thyme

½ teaspoon crushed fennel

½ teaspoon ground coriander

1 orange rind, grated

1 pinch allspice

Cook onions, carrots, and leeks in the olive oil until tender. Add remaining ingredients. Simmer this mixture for one hour; remove bay leaves. It can then be refrigerated for later use or used immediately.

About 15 minutes before serving bring the stew base to a boil and introduce 1-½ to 2 pounds of skinless, boneless mullet fillets cut into small pieces (optional: mix in other kinds of fresh seafood such as scallops, shrimp, etc.) and turn heat to low. When fish has turned opaque, stew is ready to serve. Perfect served with boiled potatoes. Serves six to eight.

Spiced-out Mullet

This recipe calls for poaching, a time-honored way to prepare our finned friends.

1-½ pounds mullet fillets

½ small onion, sliced

2 tablespoons lemon juice

10 whole cloves

¼ teaspoon salt

¼ teaspoon pepper

⅛ teaspoon red pepper

Lemon wedges

Add one inch of water to a large, deep skillet and add the first six ingredients above; mix well and bring to a boil. Reduce heat, cover and simmer a full 10 minutes. Add fish, cover and simmer 8 more minutes or until the mullet flakes easily when tested with a fork. Transfer to a warm serving platter, discarding the cooking liquid. Garnish the fish with lemon wedges and expect to be surprised at the delicate, yet spicy flavor of this dish. Serves four to six.

Flaked Mullet

Cooked, flaked mullet can be used in all sorts of recipes that call for flaked fish, even tuna!

1-½ pounds fresh mullet fillets, skinned and boned

1 quart boiling water

1 tablespoon salt

Place fillets in boiling, salted water. Cover and return to the boiling point. Reduce heat and simmer for 10 minutes or until fish flakes easily with a fork poke. Drain and flake. You should come up with something like 2 cups of flaked fish.

Yes, that white dot at center right is a jumping mullet.

Gulf Mullet Salad

Deliciously different, a recipe from state of Florida kitchens.

2-½ cups cooked, flaked mullet

2 cups cold cooked rice

1 cup chopped celery

½ cup chopped parsley

¼ cup sliced pitted ripe olives

½ cup low-fat mayonnaise

2 tablespoons low-fat French dressing

2 tablespoons lemon juice

1 teaspoon curry powder (optional)

Salad greens such as endive or Boston lettuce

Combine fish, rice, celery, parsley, and olives. Separately, combine mayonnaise, French dressing, lemon juice, and curry powder; mix thoroughly. Then add dressing to fish mixture and toss lightly; chill. Serve on salad greens. Makes six servings.

 Mountain mullet (*Agonostomus monticola*) is a related species, fairly rare, found only from North Carolina south.

Macmullet Salad

This is a real production number worth the time and effort.

  2 cups cooked, flaked mullet

  2 cups cooked shell macaroni

  1 cup chopped raw cauliflower

  1 cup sliced celery

  ¼ cup chopped parsley

  ¼ cup chopped sweet pickle or drained relish

  ½ cup low-fat mayonnaise or salad dressing

  3 tablespoons French dressing

  ⅛ teaspoon garlic juice

  1 tablespoon lemon juice

  1 teaspoon grated onion

  1 teaspoon celery seed

  ½ teaspoon salt

  ¼ teaspoon pepper

  Salad greens

  1 hard-boiled egg, sliced

Combine mullet, macaroni, cauliflower, celery, parsley, and pickle. Separately, combine mayo, French dressing, lemon juice, onion and seasonings; mix well. Add mayo mixture to mullet mixture and toss lightly; chill. Serve on salad greens. Garnish with egg slices. Serves six.

Jamaican Mullet

A subtly tangy mullet adventure

3 whole, small mullet of about ½ pound each

Olive oil

2 tablespoons chopped, peeled fresh ginger root

2 tablespoons minced, fresh chives

1 orange

Brush the cavities of the mullet with olive oil and then stuff with ginger and chives mixed. Place fish in a steamer over boiling water for about 15 to 17 minutes. Handle carefully. Remove stuffing and then tenderly, with a very sharp knife, fillet the fish. Garnish with orange slices. Serve at once to four hungry diners.

 Baby mullet eat mosquito larvae. Thus, a healthy mullet fishery means fewer biting insects.

Other Great Southern Seafood

What if, as sometimes happens, that wonderful fish the mullet is simply not available? What then? We have thoughtfully provided hand-picked recipes for the cooking of some of the mullet's closest associates in the sea. Such fish as sea trout and redfish, such shellfish as scallops and crabs, often are found in the same waters as those beautiful, bullet-headed fish of the genus *Mugil*. These perennial associates of mullet can make pretty dang good eatin' on their own. (Of course, nothing is as good as mullet and, happily, nothing can be done about *that*.)

It's probably just an interesting natural coincidence, but wherever you find mullet jumping you find other, good-to-eat fish and shellfish just hanging around! And even when the mullet are mysteriously absent, those other delicious sea critters may still be in the vicinity. Nature does provide.

So, if your seafood supplier has no mullet today, perhaps he has sea trout or scallops or blue crab. Mullet live where the water is ecologically healthy. Many other good food fish also prefer such conditions. Some of the best of these you'll have to catch yourself unless or until they go back on the commercial list. Regulations vary from state to state. Keep in close touch with those who make and change the laws regarding saltwater products. Up-to-date regs generally are available at your friendly tax collector's office, from the Marine Patrol, and at most marinas and tackle shops.

SEA TROUT

The following recipes apply especially to the spotted sea trout (*Cynoscian nebulosus*) so common in the late spring in the coastal South's saltwater bays, estuaries, and grass flats, as well as to its close relatives such as the silver and sand trout. Weakfish can be substituted with equally good results. All saltwater trout have delicate, mild-flavored flesh that fillets well but is not tolerant of rough handling.

Sea Trout Creole

A tasty item from coastal Louisiana

1 pound fresh trout fillets cut in 1-inch chunks
¼ cup canola oil
¼ cup flour
1 cup hot water
1 8-ounce can tomato sauce
3 chopped whole green onions
½ cup chopped parsley
¼ cup chopped green pepper
3 garlic cloves, finely chopped
2 red bay leaves
1-½ teaspoons salt
½ teaspoon thyme
1 dash cayenne pepper
1 slice lemon
Cooked rice

Make a traditional roux (thickened base) with oil and flour in a skillet. Stir over medium heat until reddish brown. Add water and cook and stir until smooth. Add everything else (except the rice). Cover and simmer for 17 to 22 minutes. Remove bay leaves and serve over rice. Enough for four or five diners.

Broiled Trout Wooster

A unique recipe from Texas

4 nice-sized, four- to six-ounce fresh sea trout fillets

Salt and pepper

1/3 cup olive oil

3/4 cup crunchy bread crumbs

1 teaspoon onion salt

1 teaspoon dry mustard

Dash each of Worcestershire sauce and Tabasco Sauce, combined

2 tablespoons fresh lemon juice

1 teaspoon finely chopped fresh parsley

Season the trout fillets with salt and pepper and place on a broiler pan. Brush with olive oil and broil for 4 to 5 minutes. Combine remaining oil, bread crumbs, mustard, onion salt, Worcestershire and Tabasco, lemon juice, and parsley. Generously spoon the mixture on each fillet and pat down firmly. Broil for an additional 5 to 7 minutes or until nicely browned and the trout flakes readily when tested with a fork. Good idea: Garnish with lemon slices. Serves four.

REDFISH

Sciaenops ocellatus are simply called reds, red drum, or redfish in much of the South. They are "rat reds" in Texas and "channel bass" on the Carolina coasts. It's a fish that is both easy to catch (check local regulations) and a cinch to prepare and cook with lip-smacking results.

Thanksgiving Red

1 large fresh redfish (4 to 8 pounds)

2 cups dried bread crumbs

1 large lemon, juiced and quartered

6 sprigs fresh parsley

½ cup melted butter (margarine OK)

Salt and pepper

Scale, clean and gut the whole fish. The head and tail can be left on or removed, as desired. Brush its inside with lemon juice, then with butter. Place bread crumbs and lemon quarters in food processor and process until finely mixed. Remove from processor, add parsley and just enough butter to moisten, and stir lightly. Season to taste with salt and pepper. Stuff this stuffing into the cavity of the redfish and place in a baking dish. Pour remaining melted butter over fish and bake covered at 325° F for about 18 to 23 minutes or until fish flakes easily when tested with fork. Serve on Thanksgiving with mint jelly or cranberry sauce and baked sweet potatoes. Serves six to eight.

 Mullet live to be as old as thirteen years.

Redfish Morsels

2 pounds skinned redfish fillets

1 cup all-purpose flour

1 tablespoon salt

1 teaspoon baking powder

1 cup water

1 tablespoon vinegar

Canola oil for frying

Cut fillets into one-inch cubes. Combine flour, salt, and baking powder. Slowly add water and vinegar; mix well. Dip fish cubes into batter and drop into hot (425° F) oil and cook for 2 or 3 minutes until golden brown. Drain on double layers of absorbent paper towels. Makes six to eight servings.

 Mr. Mullet was the name of a seafood restaurant (originated and co-owned by the author) in Cross City, Florida.

YELLOWTAIL (BUTTERFISH)

In many parts of the South, the tasty panfish "yellowtail" (also known as silver perch, sand perch and butterfish) is so prized by seafood epicures that fish markets carry it whenever they can buy a good catch. In other areas, this speedy, diminutive fish of silvery body and pale yellow tail is considered trash, mostly because typical specimens are only six to ten inches, rarely reaching a pound. As a "by-catch" of commercial fishing activities, the silver perch is often discarded by the thousands, which is a real shame since it is a delicious even if petite fish packed with protein and healthful oils. It is often found in the same waters frequented by mullet, particularly bays and tidal creeks.

Furthermore, even seasoned anglers admit that *Bairdiella chysoura* is surprisingly scrappy when hooked on light tackle. Though it is small, this fish is easy to fillet when the knife is sharp, the fish are cold and clamped to a cleaning board, and the lighting is good.

Perhaps one reason for the quality of yellowtail is the genetic line, it being a member of the drum family along with sea trout and reds. Here are some yellowtail recipes to do this fine little fish justice.

Yellowtail Broil

Nothing could be simpler or more delicious than this recipe for broiling in your regular oven.

4 to 8 yellowtail, depending on size

Fresh oregano

Olive oil

Lemon juice

Salt

Mrs. Dash Original Salt-Free Seasoning

Lemon wedges

Scale and gut the fish. You can leave the head, fins and tail on or remove. Preheat the broiler. Make sure the gutted fish are well rinsed. Pat dry and sprinkle the cavities with salt, Mrs. Dash, and lemon juice, and place sprigs of oregano inside. Make three diagonal cuts on the sides of each fish. Then, place the yellowtail on the broiler rack and sprinkle with olive oil and lemon juice. Broil for 6 to 8 minutes; turn, baste with oil and lemon juice, and cook another 5 to 6 minutes until crispy brown. Test with fork. When fish is properly done, diners will be able to separate flesh from bones in a single tug. Serve with lemon wedges. Serves four.

Deep-Fried Yellowtail

You'll need just a few items to create this down-home delicacy.

1-½ teaspoons adobo (Spanish seasoning consisting of salt, oregano, garlic, and black pepper)

8 yellowtail fillets, skin on

About 2 cups yellow cornmeal

Canola oil

Sprinkle adobo over each fillet; cover and leave alone in refrigerator for 60 to 90 minutes. Then, dredge the fillets in cornmeal. Carefully drop the fillets into hot (375° F) oil and fry them until they float to the top and are golden brown—like doughnuts. Drain well on double layers of paper towels and serve *with* tartar sauce and *without* delay. Feeds four or three or two. These *are* little fish.

SCALLOPS

Scallops, of course, are mussels, not fish, but they are seafood and in this author's opinion, rank among the choicest of such. Again, coincidentally, scallops often share habitat with mullet, trout, yellowtail, and all their friends. They're especially prevalent in the grass flats. Nothing sweeter than scallops comes out of salt water. (Catching scallops is quite an adventure; veteran scallopers use inner tubes, snorkel gear and wash tubs in water 2 to 6 feet deep.) Scallops are nutritious (15 percent protein!) and are easy to prepare and cook at home.

Fried Scallops

Shuck, trim and wash fresh scallops thoroughly. Sprinkle lightly with salt and pepper and then dip in cracker meal. Next put them in a mixture of beaten eggs to which has been added a small amount of table cream. (For lower fat, substitute egg whites, no cream.) Remove and dip again in the cracker crumbs. Fry in deep fat at 350° F until golden brown and tender. 10 to 15 bay scallops should serve one person.

Wicked Wokked Scallops & Veggies

Scallops, because of their relatively small size, lend themselves to quick-cooking methods, of which wok-king is one of the most fruitful. There are endless possibilities with a wok and this is just one of them.

1 pound of fresh bay scallops

1 ounce dried mushrooms

Boiling water

2 medium-sized yellow onions

4 stalks unblanched celery

8 ounces fresh green beans

5 green onions

2 tablespoons canola oil

2 teaspoons pared, grated ginger root

1 clove garlic, crushed

4 teaspoons cornstarch

1 cup water

3 tablespoons dry sherry

3 teaspoons soy sauce

2 teaspoons instant chicken bouillon granules

1 can baby corn, drained

Place the dried mushrooms in a bowl and cover with boiling water. Let stand 30 minutes. Drain. Squeeze out the water. Cut into thin slices. Rinse the scallops and drain. Trim as necessary and then cut into smaller pieces. Peel the onions, cut into wedges, and separate the layers. Cut celery into ½-inch slices. Wash and trim the beans, cutting them into 1-inch diagonal slices; cut the green onions into thin slices.

Heat oil in wok over high heat. Add the onions, celery, beans, ginger, and garlic to the oil. Stir-fry for 3 minutes.

Measure cornstarch into small bowl; blend in a few tablespoons of water and mix until smooth. Stir in remaining water, sherry, soy, and bouillon. Add to the veggie mixture. Cook and stir until mixture is boiling. Now, add scallops, mushrooms, green onions, and corn. Cook and stir until scallops are tender, about 4 and probably not more than 5 minutes. Serves four to six.

BLUE CRAB

You can buy blue crabs—fresh, live—or you can catch them. Many old-timers still get them with a stout hand line and a chicken neck, dragging the crab toward shore and nabbing it with a long-handled net. You'll have to go far to find better eating.

Ybor City Street Vendor's Crab Cakes

I confess I ate a lot of these way back when they were a dime apiece and I could eat a dollar's worth while riding my bicycle with no hands.

1 pound blue crab meat, fresh or canned (Do not use imitation.)

½ cup chopped onion

⅓ cup chopped celery

⅓ cup chopped green pepper

2 cloves garlic, minced

⅓ cup canola oil

2 cups soft bread crumbs

1 teaspoon salt

1 teaspoon prepared horseradish

1 teaspoon Worcestershire sauce

¼ teaspoon dry mustard

1 teaspoon Miracle Whip or low-fat mayonnaise

4 egg whites, beaten

1 tablespoon chopped parsley

½ teaspoon black pepper

Remove any pieces of shell or cartilage from the crab meat. Cook onion, celery, green pepper, and garlic in oil until tender but not brown. Combine all ingredients and mix well. Divide into 12 small egg-shaped cakes. Roll cakes in bread crumbs. Place cakes in heavy fry pan containing ⅛ inch hot (but not smoking) oil. Fry at moderate heat until brown on both sides. Serve with hot sauce. Enjoy! Recipe makes enough to entertain four to six persons.

Crab Stuffing

Take the crab cake recipe above and delete horseradish, Worcestershire, and mustard. Forget the little cakes and just make a crab stuffing—perfect for flounder, mullet, or redfish.

Jax Crab Bisque

1 pound fresh blue crab meat

2 tablespoons finely chopped onion

2 tablespoons finely chopped celery

¼ cup melted liquid soy-based margarine

3 tablespoons all-purpose flour

1 teaspoon salt

¼ teaspoon paprika

Dash of white pepper

1 quart milk (low-fat OK)

¼ cup chopped parsley

Remove any pieces of shell or cartilage from the crab meat. Cook onion and celery in margarine until tender but not brown. Blend in flour and seasonings. Add milk gradually, stirring constantly and cook until thick. Add crab meat and turn up heat. Do not boil. Cook until crab meat is opaque and obviously done. Just before serving, sprinkle with fresh parsley sprigs. Makes five to six servings.

SHRIMP

There are many different kinds of edible shrimp in Southern waters with at least four commercial varieties: pink, white, royal red, and brown. Shrimp is the number-one seafood item in America. Not only do humans love shrimp, fish love shrimp. So, wherever there are shrimp one is apt to find fish. Shrimp are both delicious and nutritious. A four-ounce portion delivers 23 grams of protein, no saturated fat, and some cholesterol now thought to be of a neutral or beneficial type. If you like shrimp, you'll like these recipes.

Lemon-Garlic Broiled Shrimp

This one demonstrates shrimp's astonishing versatility.

2 pounds shrimp, peeled and de-veined

2 cloves garlic, finely chopped

¼ cup margarine or butter, melted (olive oil may be substituted)

3 tablespoons lemon juice

½ teaspoon salt

⅛ teaspoon pepper

Chopped parsley (to be used as garnish)

Sauté garlic in margarine until tender but not brown. Remove from heat; add lemon juice, salt, and pepper. Arrange shrimp in a single layer in a baking dish. Pour sauce over shrimp. Broil about 4 inches from source of heat for 8 to 10 minutes or until shrimp are no longer translucent in the center. Baste once during broiling. Garnish with fresh parsley. Serves six.

Lafayette Seafood Gumbo

There are gumbo recipes and gumbo recipes. On a scale of one to ten, we put this very traditional Louisiana version at 9-½.

1 pound cooked, unpeeled shrimp (You'll be saving the peels.)

1 3-ounce bag shrimp and crab boil (We recommend Zatarain's brand.)

5 cups water

4 tablespoons butter (olive oil can be substituted)

1 onion, peeled and finely sliced

1 bell pepper, cut into small pieces

2 garlic cloves, finely chopped

4 tablespoons all-purpose flour

½ teaspoon thyme

1 bay leaf

2 tablespoons chopped fresh parsley

¼ teaspoon Worcestershire sauce

12 fresh, just-shelled oysters

8 ounces peeled, chopped tomatoes

2 tablespoons ground sassafras leaves (known in Cajun country as filé, a flavorful thickener)

Salt and pepper

Freshly cooked rice

Start by peeling the shrimp, of course. Save the shells, including the legs and heads if you have them, adding them to the water, along with the crab/shrimp boil bag. Bring the combination to a boil in a large cooking pot. Reduce heat and simmer for 18 to 22 minutes. Then, in another pot melt the butter (or heat the oil), and once it bubbles add the onion, green pepper, garlic, and flour. Cook slowly, stirring constantly until the flour is a pleasant golden brown. Slowly strain in the seasoned shrimp stock; discard the shells and pieces. Add the thyme and bay leaf. Stir well, bringing the mixture to a boil. Reduce heat and simmer until thick.

Add the parsley and Worcestershire sauce. Put in the fresh oysters and peeled shrimp along with the tomatoes and heat through until the oysters and shrimp are fully cooked. Add filé powder and leave the concoction to thicken. Before serving remove the bay leaf. Serve over cooked rice. Serves six to eight.

Escambian Spaghetti

The only "crawk pawt" recipe in this book, this one earns its place by virtue of simplicity and exciting taste. Try it, whatever brand of electric slow cooker you may happen to own.

1 16-ounce can cut tomatoes (We recommend using a quality brand.)

2 tablespoons minced parsley

1 garlic clove, minced

½ teaspoon dried basil

1 teaspoon salt

¼ teaspoon fresh ground black pepper

1 teaspoon dried oregano

1 6-ounce can tomato paste (We recommend using a quality brand.)

½ teaspoon Mrs. Dash Original Seasoning

1 pound boiled, shelled shrimp

Grated Parmesan cheese

Cooked spaghetti

In a crock pot combine the tomatoes, parsley, garlic, basil, salt, pepper, oregano, tomato paste, and Mrs. Dash. Cook on low with cover on for 6 to 7 hours. Turn temperature up to high and carefully add the shrimp, mixing gently; cover and cook on high for 10 to 15 minutes. Serve the mixture, topped with the grated cheese, over hot, cooked spaghetti. Serves four.

Mullet of the Future

The sea abounds in wonderful food for human consumption. The food is good because we have found ways to make it highly palatable, and it is good because we have discovered its significant health benefits. The health mandate, *Eat More Seafood*, is the basis of a whole lifestyle that many respected medical authorities are encouraging us to take seriously. Why not live longer and healthier while, and partially as a consequence of, eating some of the best-tasting food available on the planet?

Mullet is one brightly shining example of high quality, tasty and nutritious seafood. But there are many others, as the present book hints at from time to time even while a certain understandable bias may be detected. This bias is because for unique savor and healthy components, mullet is very hard to beat.

What the author hopes is this: That the mullet resource will become stronger with necessary protection and management by appropriate agencies. That commercial fishermen will use cast nets and other highly efficient, virtually species-specific devices to harvest mullet. That the consumer will continue to value the mullet at the level it surely deserves. Furthermore, that mullet aquaculture be considered seriously.

I also hope everybody who acquires *The Mostly Mullet Cookbook* will give all its recipes a try and feel free to provide candid feedback or recipe contributions toward any future revisions. May there be plenty of fresh mullet in our future.

George "Grif" Griffin
P.O. Box 81
Old Town, FL 32680-0081

Index